The Effective Teacher's Guide to Autism and Communication Difficulties

Nearly one in ten children experience some difficulty communicating. These children may really struggle to understand what people are saying to them and have difficulty expressing their feelings and thoughts.

The Effective Teacher's Guide to Autism and Communication Difficulties examines the causes and consequences of communication difficulties and autism. Focusing on educational aspects, the book pays particular attention to difficulties teachers may encounter with speech, grammar, meaning, use of language and comprehension. This practical, teacher-friendly book clearly and concisely leads the reader through:

◆ terms and definitions
◆ legal considerations
◆ classroom strategies
◆ pedagogical issues.

Highly accessible and authoritative, this book is a rich source of knowledge and is full of ideas and guidance on how to achieve good practice in the classroom. It is essential reading for any teacher or practitioner striving to enhance the educational prospects of pupils.

Michael Farrell is an independent educational consultant and recognised expert in special education. He has written or edited over 30 acclaimed education books.

New Directions in Special Educational Needs

By focusing firmly on what really works in practice with children with special educational needs, this highly practical series will enlighten and inform any busy teacher eager to know more about individual difficulties, and who wants to make inclusion a reality for their pupils.

All books in the series concentrate on the educational implications of certain special educational needs. They also consider the legal obligations of schools, what teachers can do to support and encourage inclusive learning in their classroom, and where they can go for additional support and advice. Packed full of down-to-earth yet authoritative advice, this series will provide teachers with everything they need to ensure their pupils with special educational needs are effectively and properly supported.

Titles in the Series (all by Michael Farrell)

The Effective Teacher's Guide to Behavioural, Emotional and Social Difficulties
Practical strategies

The Effective Teacher's Guide to Autism and Communication Difficulties
Practical strategies

The Effective Teacher's Guide to Dyslexia and Other Specific Learning Difficulties
Practical strategies

The Effective Teacher's Guide to Moderate, Severe and Profound Learning Difficulties
Practical strategies

The Effective Teacher's Guide to Sensory Impairment and Physical Disability
Practical strategies

The Effective Teacher's Guide to Autism and Communication Difficulties

Practical strategies

Michael Farrell

Routledge
Taylor & Francis Group

LONDON AND NEW YORK

First published 2006
by Routledge
2 Park Square, Milton Park, Abingdon, Oxon OX14 4RN

Simultaneously published in the USA and Canada
by Routledge
270 Madison Ave, New York, NY 10016

Routledge is an imprint of the Taylor & Francis Group

© 2006 Michael Farrell

Typeset in Times New Roman and Gill by
Florence Production Ltd, Stoodleigh, Devon
Printed and bound in Great Britain by
Bell & Bain Ltd, Glasgow

British Library Cataloguing in Publication Data
A catalogue record for this book is available from the British Library

Library of Congress Cataloging in Publication Data
A catalog record has been requested for this book

ISBN10: 0–415–36039–0

ISBN13: 9–78–0–415–36039–5

Contents

Abbreviations

AFASIC	Association For All Speech Impaired Children
ASD	autistic spectrum disorders
ASDS	*Asperger's Syndrome Diagnostic Scale*
BSL	British Sign Language
CELF	*Clinical Evaluation of Language Fundamentals Test*
CFT	communication facilitation techniques
CHAT	*Checklist for Autism in Toddlers*
DfEE	Department for Education and Employment
DfES	Department for Education and Skills
DoH	Department of Health
DSM-IV-TR	*Diagnostic and Statistical Manual of Mental Disorders – Fourth Edition, Text Revision*
DVD	developmental verbal dyspraxia
ESPP	Early Support Pilot Programme
GADS	*Gilliam Asperger's Disorder Scale*
GARS	*Gilliam Autism Rating Scale*
IEP	individual education plan
LARSP	*Language Assessment, Remediation and Screening Procedure*
LEA	local education authority
LSA	learning support assistant
MLU	mean length of utterance
PDD.NOS	pervasive developmental disorder. Not otherwise specified
PECS	Picture Exchange Communication System
PIPA	*Preschool and Primary Inventory of Phonological Awareness*
PLASC	Pupil Level Annual School Census
QCA	Qualifications and Curriculum Authority
SALT	speech and language therapist
SEN	special educational needs
SENCO	special educational needs co-ordinator
ST	'structured teaching'
SULP	*Social Use of Language Programme*
TEACCH	Treatment and Education of Autistic and related Communication handicapped CHildren
TOAL	*Test of Adolescent and Adult Language*
TOLD	*Test of Language Development*

Acknowledgement

I am most grateful to Andrew Burnett, Chief Therapist (Education), Children's Speech and Language Service, Plymouth, for reading an earlier manuscript and making many helpful suggestions.

Dr Michael Farrell trained as a teacher and as a psychologist at the Institute of Psychiatry and has worked as a head teacher, a lecturer at the Institute of Education, London and as a local education authority inspector. He managed national projects for City University and for the Government Department of Education. Michael Farrell presently works as an independent educational consultant. This has involved policy development and training with LEAs, work with voluntary organisations, support to schools in the independent and maintained sectors, and advice to ministries abroad. Among his numerous books, which are translated into European and Asian languages, are:

Key Issues for Primary Schools (Routledge, 1999)

Key Issues for Secondary Schools (Routledge, 2001)

Understanding Special Educational Needs: A Guide for Student Teachers (Routledge, 2003)

Key Issues in Special Education (Routledge, 2005)

Chapter 1

Communication and interaction difficulties

INTRODUCTION

To communicate and to interact is of such central importance, not only in education but in everyday life, that it will be apparent that, where a child or young person experiences significant difficulties in these areas, it is essential that suitable educational provision is put in place to help ensure that the pupil makes the best progress possible.

This chapter sets the book in the context of the 'New Directions in Special Educational Needs' series, of which it forms a part. It outlines the contents of the book, chapter by chapter, and describes the proposed readers. I then define communication and interaction difficulties and describe pupils considered to have them. This is done with reference to the *Special Educational Needs Code of Practice* (DfES, 2001); the guidance, *Data Collection by Type of Special Educational Needs* (DfES, 2003); and the legal definition of special educational needs (SEN). The sort of provision from which pupils with communication and interaction difficulties appear to benefit is touched upon. The chapter considers the prevalence of communication and interaction difficulties. I mention the range of provision for pupils. Finally, the chapter outlines the issues of professionals working closely together, working with parents, and involving pupils.

The place of this book in the New Directions in Special Educational Needs series and an outline of the chapter contents

This book, *The Effective Teacher's Guide to Autism and Communication and Interaction Difficulties,* is part of a 'New Directions in Special Educational Needs' series covering the types of SEN related to those outlined in the *Special Educational Needs Code of Practice* (DfES, 2001). The series focuses on what works in the education of pupils with SEN. It covers:

◆ behavioural, emotional and social difficulties;
◆ general learning difficulties (moderate, severe, and profound and multiple learning difficulties);

◆   specific learning difficulties (dyslexia, dyspraxia, dyscalculia);
◆   communication and interaction difficulties (speech, language and communication difficulties; autistic spectrum disorders (ASD));
◆   sensory and physical difficulties (visual impairment, hearing impairment, multi-sensory impairment, physical disability).

The present book covers:

Chapter 2: Difficulties with speech

This explains the speech elements of phonology, phonetics and prosody. It examines the nature and causes of phonological, phonetic and prosodic difficulties. I look at the identification and assessment of speech difficulties. The chapter then examines interventions, including speech and language therapy advice and intervention and raising phonological awareness.

Chapter 3: Difficulties with grammar

This chapter explains what grammar is and distinguishes syntax and morphology. I consider difficulties with grammar. The chapter looks at the identification and assessment of difficulties with grammar. Interventions are explained, such as the teacher ensuring that her communication is direct and clear and supporting the development of grammatical utterances through reading and writing activities.

Chapter 4: Difficulties with meaning

This chapter considers the development of an understanding of meaning in terms of labelling, packaging, networking, understanding idiom, understanding grammar and understanding the meaning of relations. The identification and assessment of these aspects is considered and related interventions such as the use of structured experiences are outlined.

Chapter 5: Difficulties with the use of language

I look at the use of language (pragmatics) in this chapter in terms of grammatical sense in language use, and at social and linguistic sense. I consider conversational skill then look at difficulties in these areas. The chapter examines identification and assessment in relation to pragmatics. I examine interventions such as developing conversational skills and helping the child with difficulties in social and linguistic sense.

Chapter 6: Difficulties with comprehension

This chapter explains what is meant by language comprehension and examines the roles of attention and grammar in relation to comprehension. I look at difficulties with comprehension and at their identification and assessment. Interventions discussed include the modelling of listening behaviour and encouraging pupils' assertiveness to signal a lack of understanding.

Chapter 7: Provision for pupils with autistic spectrum disorders

In this chapter I define autism and ASD, with reference to a triad of impairments in terms of social isolation, communication difficulties and insistence on sameness. I also look at issues of identification and assessment and outline a range of interventions, such as the Lovaas programme and the Picture Exchange Communication System (PECS).

Chapter 8: Conclusion

The final chapter draws together threads from earlier chapters.

Each chapter has its own introduction and headings and ends with thinking points and recommended key texts. At the end of the book are a list of physical and internet addresses, a bibliography and a combined subject and author index.

Proposed readers

The book is intended particularly for the following readers:

◆ all teachers, SEN co-ordinators (SENCOs) and head teachers in mainstream schools and units working with pupils with communication and interaction difficulties;
◆ all staff in special schools providing for pupils with communication and inter-action difficulties;
◆ local education authority (LEA) officers with an interest in and/or responsibility for pupils with communication and interaction difficulties;
◆ student teachers and newly qualified teachers wishing to gain an understanding of educational provision for pupils with communication and interaction difficulties;
◆ teachers and others undergoing continuing professional development;
◆ school advisers and inspectors.

What are communication and interaction difficulties?

The Special Educational Needs Code of Practice

As a starting point, the *Special Educational Needs Code of Practice* (DfES, 2001) indicates that, 'Most children with special educational needs have strengths and difficulties in one, some or all of the areas of speech, language and communication' (Chapter 7: section 55). The range of difficulties will encompass children and young people with:

◆ speech and language delay, impairments or disorders;
◆ specific learning difficulties;
◆ autistic spectrum disorders;
◆ sensory impairment, e.g. hearing impairment;
◆ physical impairment.

(7: 55, paraphrased)

Such speech, language and communication difficulties 'may' (7: 56) apply to some children with general learning difficulties (moderate, severe or profound).

Possible triggers for intervention at the level of Early Years Action include 'the practitioner's or parent's concern about a child who, despite receiving appropriate educational experiences . . . has communication and/or interaction difficulties, and requires specific individual interventions in order to access learning' (4: 21).

In the case of Early Years Action Plus, the triggers for seeking help outside the school could be that 'despite receiving an individualised programme and/or concentrated support, the child . . . has ongoing communication or interaction difficulties that impede the development of social relationships and cause substantial barriers to learning' (4: 31).

In the primary phase, the triggers for School Action could be 'the teacher's or others' concern, underpinned by evidence, about a child, who despite receiving differentiated learning opportunities . . . has communication and/or interaction difficulties, and continues to make little or no progress despite the provision of specialist equipment' (5: 44). School Action Plus triggers in the primary phase could be that, 'despite receiving an individualised programme and/or concentrated support under School Action, the child . . . has ongoing communication or interaction difficulties that impede the development of social relationships and cause substantial barriers to learning' (5: 56).

Turning to the secondary sector, School Action triggers (6: 51) and School Action Plus triggers (6: 64) are almost identical to those for the primary phase.

Regarding the statutory assessment of SEN, when an LEA is deciding whether to carry out an assessment, it should 'seek evidence of any identifiable factors that could impact on learning outcomes including . . . significant delays in language functioning . . . any evidence of impaired social interaction or communication or a significantly restricted repertoire of activities, interests and imaginative development' (7: 43)

The guidance, Data Collection by Type of Special Educational Needs

A further description of 'communication and interaction needs' is provided in the guidance, *Data Collection by Type of Special Educational Needs* connected with the Pupil Level Annual School Census (PLASC) (DfES, 2003) (www.dfes.gov. uk/sen). The Department for Education and Skills (DfES) sent original draft descriptions to a sample of schools, LEAs and voluntary organisations and amended them in the light of the comments received. Communication and interaction needs are considered under two sections: speech, language and communication needs; and ASD.

Speech, language and communication needs

Pupils with speech, language and communication needs are only recorded for the purposes of the PLASC if 'additional educational provision is being made to help them access the curriculum' (p. 3). Such pupils:

> may have difficulty in understanding and/or making others understand information conveyed through spoken language. Their acquisition of speech and

their oral language skills may be significantly behind their peers. Their speech may be poor or unintelligible. Pupils with speech difficulties may experience problems in articulation and the production of speech sounds. They may have severe stammer.

Pupils with language impairments may find it hard to understand and/or use words in context. They may use words incorrectly with inappropriate grammatical patterns, have a reduced vocabulary or find it hard to recall words and express ideas. They may also hear or see a word but not be able to understand its meaning or have trouble getting others to understand what they are trying to say.

(p. 5)

The kinds of difficulty experienced relate to subsequent chapters of the present book. These include: problems with speech, including 'articulation and the production of speech sounds' (Chapter 2); grammar such as 'inappropriate grammatical patterns' (Chapter 3); meaning (Chapter 4); language use (Chapter 5); and understanding (Chapter 6).

Autistic spectrum disorders

The guidance, *Data Collection by Type of Special Educational Needs* (DfES, 2003), points out that pupils should only be recorded as ASD for the purposes of the PLASC if 'additional educational provision is being made to help them access the curriculum' (p. 3). Pupils with ASD cover 'the full range of ability' and the severity of the impairment 'varies widely'. Some pupils have 'learning disabilities', adding to the difficulties of diagnosis. The guidance states that pupils with ASD find it difficult to:

◆ understand and use non-verbal and verbal communication
◆ understand social behaviour – which affects their ability to interact with children and adults
◆ think and behave flexibly – which may be shown in restricted, obsessional or repetitive activities.

(p. 5)

Elaborating on the three criteria (which form the basis of most definitions and are sometimes called the 'triad' of impairment), the guidance explains that pupils with ASD may 'have difficulty in understanding the communication of others and in developing effective communication themselves. Many are delayed in learning to speak and some never develop meaningful speech' (p. 5).

Turning to the social difficulty aspect of ASD, the guidance mentions the difficulty pupils have in understanding the social behaviour of others. It states: 'They are literal thinkers and fail to understand the social context. They can experience high levels of stress and anxiety in settings that don't [*sic*] meet their needs or when routines are changed. This can lead to inappropriate behaviour' (p. 5).

Regarding the difficulty of thinking and behaving flexibly, the guidance observes that; 'Young pupils may not play with toys in a conventional or imaginative way but instead use toys rigidly or repetitively. . . . They find it hard to generalise skills and have difficulty adapting to new situations and often prefer routine' (p. 6).

Reflecting developments in the understanding of ASD that extend the usual triad of impairment, the guidance notes that some pupils with ASD have different perceptions of senses. (This can lead to some children finding certain sounds and noises very unpleasant, for example.)

Communication and interaction difficulties and the legal definition of SEN

Communication and interaction difficulties can also be understood by examining them in the context of the legal definition of SEN in the Education Act 1996. The Act provides a layered definition in which a 'difficulty in learning' or a 'disability' may lead to a 'learning difficulty', which may call for special educational provision to be made, therefore constituting an SEN.

In this context, speech, language and communication difficulties would be manifested as difficulties in learning or developing speech, grammar, understanding of the meaning of words, the use of language and comprehension, such that a child's attainment in these areas is lower than that of other children of the same age. The 'difficulty in learning' in relation to these areas is of such significance that there is a 'learning difficulty' that calls for special educational provision to be made, therefore constituting a special educational need. ASD can be viewed similarly in that the development of communication, social understanding and flexible behaviour are at lower levels than those of children of the same age. This does not, however, quite capture the particular difficulties of ASD, which are often very subtle. Other definitions of difficulties with speech, grammar, meaning, language use and comprehension and of ASD are provided in subsequent chapters.

Provision for pupils with communication and interaction difficulties

The present section seeks to indicate something more about the nature of communication and interaction difficulties by touching on the interventions that are used when educating pupils with them. As a starting point, the *Special Educational Needs Code of Practice* (DfES, 2001) provides a basic description of provision from which pupils with communication and interaction difficulties may benefit. They may require:

- help in acquiring, comprehending and using language;
- help in articulation;
- help in acquiring literacy skills;
- help in using augmentative and alternative means of communication;
- help in using different means of communication confidently and competently for a range of purposes, including formal situations;

- help in organising and co-ordinating oral and written language;
- support to compensate for the impact of a communication difficulty on learning in English as an additional language;
- help in expressing, comprehending and using their own language, where English is not the first language.

(7: 56)

Guidance connected with the PLASC (DfES, 2003) (www.dfes.gov.uk/sen) indicates that pupils should only be recorded as having communication and interaction difficulties 'if additional educational provision is being made to help them to access the curriculum' (p. 4).

Causation and prevalence of communication and interaction difficulties

Subsequent chapters consider the possible causes of difficulties with speech, grammar, meaning, language use and comprehension.

The prevalence of speech and language difficulties is hard to estimate. Among the reasons are that there is such a wide range of difficulties and that there are different views about the level at which they are considered to be significant enough to require special educational provision. One view is that perhaps one in ten children have language and communication needs (Law *et al.*, 2000a). Boys are more likely to be identified than girls, often quoted ratios being 3:1 or 4:1.

Government statistics regarding 'speech, language and communication needs', in January 2004 in England (DfES, 2004, table 9), indicated that there were 40,570 at School Action Plus representing 11.5 per cent of pupils at this part of the SEN framework and a further 23,320 pupils with statements of SEN or 9.9 per cent of pupils with statements. In primary schools, 36,040 of these pupils were at School Action Plus (16.5 per cent of all pupils at School Action Plus in primary schools) and 14,080 had statements of SEN (20.5 per cent of all pupils with statements in primary schools). In secondary schools, the number was much smaller, being 4,400 at School Action Plus (3.3 per cent) and 6,320 with statements of SEN (8.1 per cent). In special schools, where it is much less usual for pupils not to have statements of SEN, there were only 130 pupils at School Action Plus (7.8 per cent) and 2,910 with statements of SEN (3.3 per cent). The figures for special schools included pupils attending maintained and non-maintained special schools but excluded pupils in independent special schools and pupils in maintained hospital schools.

The possible causes of and the prevalence of ASD are discussed in Chapter 7.

Inclusion and communication and interaction difficulties

One understanding of inclusion is that it aims to encourage schools to reconsider their structure, teaching approaches, pupil grouping and use of support so that the school responds to the perceived needs of all its pupils. Teachers, collaborating closely, seek opportunities to look at new ways of involving all pupils and to draw on experimentation and reflection. There should be planned access to a broad and balanced curriculum developed from its foundations as a curriculum for all pupils.

A view of inclusion is that it concerns educating an increasing number of pupils in mainstream schools and fewer and perhaps eventually none in special schools and other venues. Other views include that it is about pupils receiving a good education, whether that is in a special school or a mainstream school. Indeed, the Qualifications and Curriculum Authority (QCA) have characterised inclusion as 'securing appropriate opportunities for learning, assessment and qualifications to enable the full and effective participation of all pupils in the process of learning' (Wade, 1999). In this context, pupils with severe speech and language difficulties may be taught in special schools such as those managed by the charity I-CAN, or in maintained special schools, while others attend units in mainstream schools and yet others attend mainstream school classrooms full-time. Similarly, with pupils with ASD, there is a range of provision including special schools under the auspices of the National Autistic Society, LEAs and others, specially resourced units in mainstream schools and mainstream class placements.

Professionals working closely together

While exhortations for professionals to work closely together are frequent in government documents, the practicalities are constantly challenging. Professionals involved with children with communication and interaction difficulties may include the teacher, the general practitioner, speech and language therapist (SALT), school medical officer, educational psychologist, teaching assistant, advisory teacher and others. Each may have a different professional perspective and a different level of experience concerning communication and interaction difficulties.

Particular challenges have been recognised where professionals working in schools are line-managed by different services. SALTs, for example, may work full-time in a school or several schools but be employed by the health services. For multi-professional working to be practicable, clear lines of communication are necessary and a structure that demarcates responsibility without being too constraining. Among initiatives to encourage effective joint working is the *Joint Professional Development Framework* (I-CAN, 2001). This sets out a structure to underpin joint training arrangements for teachers and SALTs working with children with speech, language and communication needs.

Early years development and childcare partnerships use interagency planning to bring together early years education and social care. Health action zones and education action zones co-ordinate action on social disadvantage and social support for pupils with SEN. SEN regional partnerships have encouraged discussions and joint planning between education, health and social services on some topics. Aspects of the 'Excellence in Cities' programme included encouraging school-based learning support units, working with pupils at risk of exclusion from school, to work with learning mentors and out-of-school support services. The Sure Start initiative offered the opportunity to interrelate family policy and the early identification and support of pupils with SEN.

In 2003, an Early Support Pilot Programme (ESPP) for the families of children aged 0 to 3 years with complex needs was designed to develop good service provision and to support development in various areas, including the co-ordination of multi-agency support for families and partnership across agencies and geographical boundaries. This involved joint work between the DfES and others, including the Royal National Institute for the Blind, the Royal National Institute for the Deaf and the National Children's Bureau (www.earlysupport.org.uk). See also the DfES website (www.dfes.gov.uk/sen), the Department of Health (DoH) website (www.doh.gov.uk) or the National Children's Bureau website (www.ncb.org.uk).

Related to joint professional working, a National Children's Trust Framework was announced in 2001 intended to develop new standards across the National Health Service and social services for children and encourage partnership between agencies. Children's Trusts were subsequently seen as seeking to integrate local education, social care and some health services (through the Health Act 1999, section 31) for children and young people and to incorporate an integrated commissioning strategy. The LEA will include potentially all education functions, including special educational needs (SEN), the education welfare service and educational psychology. Children's social services will include assessment and services for children 'in need'. Community and acute health services will include locally provided and commissioned child and adolescent mental health services and could also include speech and language therapy, health visiting, physiotherapy and occupational therapy services concerned with children and families. (Primary Care Trusts will be able to delegate functions into the Children's Trust and will be able to pool funds with the local authority.)

Trusts can also include other services such as Connexions, Youth Offending teams and Sure Start. Local partners such as the police, voluntary organisations, housing services and leisure services can be involved. Children's Trusts are expected to sit within local authorities reporting to the director of children's services, who in turn will report to the chief executive to the local councillors. The Children's Trusts will commission services and may provide these directly or by contracts through public, private or voluntary sector organisations.

The resulting integration of service provision is expected to be reflected in such features as: co-located services such as Children's Centres and extended schools; multi-disciplinary teams and a key worker system; a common assessment framework across services; information-sharing systems across services; joint training; and effective arrangements for safeguarding children. The intention was to integrate key children's services within a single organisational focus, preferably through Children's Trusts. Bids for 35 'Pathfinder' Trusts were approved in 2003, funded to 2006 (www.doh.gov.uk/nsf/children/index.htm).

Working with parents

Working closely with parents is an aspiration of all schools and a continuing theme in government guidance. The *Special Educational Needs Code of Practice* (DfES, 2001) devotes a chapter to 'Working in Partnership with Parents' and specific guidance on seeking to understand what parents might need is available (e.g. Greenwood, 2002). The perspectives on communication and interaction difficulties assume that parents are as fully involved as is practicable. The school's support of parents may include:

- providing information about SEN and practical strategies for coping;
- putting parents in touch with support groups, locally and nationally;
- making school premises available for various activities, such as a parents' support group;
- having displays of literature such as leaflets;
- being a 'one stop' point of contact for other services.

A model for collaborating with parents in order to help pupils experiencing difficulties at school is suggested by Hornby (2003, p. 131), and may have wider application for work with parents of pupils with SEN generally. It distinguishes between what it is considered parents 'need' and what they can reasonably be expected to contribute.

Parents' *needs* are considered to be communication with the school (which all parents need); liaison such as that taking place at parent–teacher meetings (which most parents need); education such as parents' workshops (which many need); and support such as counselling (which some need).

Parents' *contributions* are considered as relating to information, for example about the child's strengths (which all parents can provide); collaboration, for example with supporting a pupil's individual education plan (IEP) (to which most parents could contribute); resources, such as being a classroom aid (which many could contribute); and helping develop policy, for example being a parent governor of the school (which some could contribute).

The model leaves open the exact interpretation of what the expressions 'most', 'many' and 'some' might mean and schools will bring their own judgements to bear on, for example, whether it is reasonable to expect 'many' parents to contribute at a level suggested by being a classroom aid. Nevertheless the basic structure of the model with a graduated view of the parents' proposed needs and their potential contribution is a helpful one.

Among particular programmes intended to support the parents of children with communication difficulties are *Child's Talk* (Aldred *et al.*, 2001) and *Early Bird*, for the carers of children diagnosed with ASD and aged 0 to 3 years (Shields, 2001).

Involving pupils

Materials used when seeking to explore the views of children with learning difficulties include such sources as: the guidelines, *Listening to Children with Communication Support Needs* (Aitken and Millar, 2002) and *How It Is* (Marchant and Cross, 2002); and projects such as *Can You Hear Us?: Including the Views of Disabled Children and Young People* (Whittles, 1998). Lewis (2004) lists some aspects of methods relevant to chronologically young children or 'developmentally young' children. These include:

- permit or encourage 'don't know' responses and requests for clarification;
- stress not knowing the events or views of the child to counter the child's assumption that the adult knows the answer (the child tends to be more suggestible if the adult has credibility and rapport with the child);
- use statements rather than questions to trigger fuller responses from children;

- if using questions, use an appropriate level of generality (for example 'open or moderately focused questions seem to generate more accurate responses from children with learning difficulties than do highly specific questions');
- avoid 'yes/no' questions to avoid acquiescence, particularly for pupils with learning difficulties;
- aim for an uninterrupted narrative.

(Lewis, 2004, pp. 4–6 paraphrased)

At the whole-school level, all pupils may have the opportunity to be involved in such structures as a school council in which pupil representatives of each class or other grouping in the school discuss matters of concern to all pupils and staff.

The *Special Educational Needs Code of Practice* (DfES, 2001, especially Chapter 3) encourages pupil participation and intimates that pupils, including those with communication and interaction difficulties, should be involved in the development and evaluations of IEPs, where possible.

Beyond this, the fullest practicable involvement of the pupil in his education should be sought. Pupils should be part of the process of assessment and the purpose of any assessment and how it is intended the assessment will benefit the pupils' education should be explained. The results of assessment and what it might mean should be discussed. Where pupils are fully involved in setting their own targets for learning, they are more likely to strive to reach them. Pupils are also usefully involved in their own annual reviews of progress. A balance is sought between encouraging participation and overburdening the pupil when he may not have sufficient experience and knowledge to make judgements without support.

THINKING POINT

Readers may wish to consider with reference to a particular school:

- the effectiveness of procedures for seeking a commonly held understanding of communication and interaction difficulties, such as discussion, consultation with the SENCO and observation of pupils.

KEY TEXTS

Farrell, M. (2003) *Special Education Handbook* (3rd edn), London, David Fulton Publishers.

As a starting point, this book provides entries on various topics relating to communication and interaction difficulties. These include: 'speech and language therapist', 'speech and language therapy', 'sign language' and 'symbols'. Appendices summarise legislation and related reports and consultative documents from the 'Warnock report' to the present day; selected regulations from 1981 to the present; and selected circulars and circular letters from 1981 to the present, including the *Special Educational Needs Code of Practice* of 2001 and the Special Educational Needs and Disability Act 2001.

––––––––––––

Thompson, G. (2003) *Supporting Children with Communication Disorders: A Handbook for Teachers and Teaching Assistants*, London, David Fulton Publishers.

This provides a brief and readable overview of communication difficulties with a passing mention of ASD.

––––––––––––

Chapter 2

Difficulties with speech

INTRODUCTION

This chapter considers and explains the interrelated speech elements of phonetics, prosody and phonology and examines the nature and causes of phonetic, prosodic and phonological difficulties. I look at the identification and assessment of speech difficulties in terms of liaison between the teacher, the SENCO and the SALT; screening procedures; assessment in different language contexts; and distinguishing between speech difficulties and grammar difficulties. The chapter then examines several interventions and their rationale, including SALT advice and intervention, raising phonological awareness, and error analysis and articulation exercises. I examine individual task-based programmes, communication through methods other than speech, and, briefly, medical/surgical interventions.

The chapter also considers behavioural, emotional and social difficulties that may arise with pupils having severe speech difficulties and finally touches on the assessment of speech difficulties for children for whom English is an additional language.

Phonetics, prosody and phonology

The terms 'speech' and 'language' may be differentiated in that one can have language without speech as in manual sign language. As Martin and Miller (2003) state, 'speech is only one form of language. It is a way of using the sounds of the human voice to communicate. We can also use writing, or signs. Speech is the audible (spoken) form of language' (p. 2). In another context, assuming that speech refers to language, Thompson defines speech as 'the mechanical aspect of communication . . . the ability to produce the sounds, words and phrases' (2003, p. 1).

Phonetics, prosody and phonology are interrelated aspects of speech that are considered separately below, in part to make explanation easier and in part because causation and intervention sometimes relate to one aspect more specifically than another.

Phonetics

Phonetics is the study of articulation. Articulation is the form of motor skill learning that leads to the automatic moving of speech articulators in the mouth in 'rapid, precise and co-ordinated sequences' (Martin and Miller, 2003, p. 37). Similarly, articulation has been described as 'the motor process of speech production' and the accurate and precise movement and co-ordination of the organs of articulation (e.g. tongue, jaw, teeth and lips) to produce sounds (Thompson, 2003, p. 1). Phonetic aspects of speech include the speech sounds that can be segmented into the components of their articulation and into consonants and vowels.

Prosody

Prosody is an aspect of phonetics but may be differentiated in that it refers to features of speech such as volume, patterns of intonation and changes in pitch that indicate questions, feeling, surprise and so on. Also, the rhythm and fluency of speech help convey meaning and consequently aid the understanding of the listener. When learning a new word, speakers attend particularly to the opening consonant(s) of a syllable (the 'onset') and to the beat of the syllables. It follows from this that, when teaching children new vocabulary, it is helpful to them to draw particular attention to these two features. Prosodic aspects of speech can affect the meaning of a complete utterance, as when the intonation is raised at the end of an utterance to indicate a question. In such an instance, this has an effect at the phonological level of speech, which is considered in the next section.

Phonology

Broadly, phonology refers to 'all the sound related aspects of language, knowledge and behaviour' (Watson, 1991, p. 26). More specifically, phonology has to do with the differences in speech sounds that carry meaning. It is 'the system with rules to organise speech sounds into sequences to make words' (Martin, 2000, p. 14). When a child's speech difficulty concerns phonology there is a difficulty in relating speech sounds to changes in meaning.

It is phonological knowledge that enables the speaker to understand that, when a speech sound is changed in a word, meaning changes. A German friend of mine who, in a card game, having not sufficiently internalised the pertinent sounds of 'aces' and on one occasion announcing to his astonished fellow players that he had 'three arses', had not quite grasped this distinction in English. More commonly, speakers in their own language come to learn distinctions such as 'dog'/'log' or 'pig'/'pin'. The speaker hears her own speech and modifies it as necessary to make the required word.

The phonological system is considered to lay down a sort of cognitive phonological representation of the speech–sound sequence, which is in part what enables the process to be automatic. Speakers can draw on this phonological representation when they are developing awareness of the different sounds in a word. (In reading in English, the 44 speech sounds are linked to written marks or graphemes so that the child develops a phoneme–grapheme correspondence).

Children develop their speech sound system 'through a series of phonological processes, based on rules that affect the sounds and syllables in words and that make their early words easier to say' (Martin, 2000, p. 15). For example, a young child may reduce several consonants to one consonant, making 'brick' into 'bick'. Speech sound development is typically such that approximately 90 per cent of a child's speech is intelligible to a stranger by the time the child is 4 years old (Law *et al.*, 2000b, p. 18).

Speech difficulties: their nature and causes

Speech difficulties can be said to occur when communication is impaired by the child's capacity for speech.

Physical factors can affect speech at different levels. Neurological damage such as head injury in an accident or brain damage before, during or soon after birth can in some instances lead to physical disabilities with associated speech difficulties. Neurological disease such as brain tumours or meningitis can be associated with speech difficulties, which may be progressive. Speech difficulties related to neurological damage or to disease are covered by the term 'dysarthria'. For example, poor motor skills and poor co-ordination can lead to slurred articulation. Such neurologically based speech difficulties may be so severe that they call for the use of non-speech-based communication.

Developmental verbal dyspraxia (DVD) is thought to relate to immature neural development, though this is an area of debate. Sometimes known as apraxia of speech and as a disorder of motor planning, it affects a child's ability to co-ordinate the speech organs in order to produce speech accurately. Because the child with DVD has difficulty with speech, especially at speed, he may avoid speaking and will need support and encouragement. The child requires much practice before being able to 'incorporate new sounds into syllables and words at normal speed' (Kirby and Drew, 2003, p. 135). Conversational and other pressures may adversely affect a child's performance. Among the indications of DVD are:

◆ 'the child may produce few consonants correctly and find it difficult to imitate tongue and lip movements or sounds in isolation' (Thompson, 2003, p. 66);
◆ 'speech production may require a greater effort from the child and sounds may be difficult to distinguish' (p. 66);
◆ speech may be 'slow or halting, and sometimes it appears to be a struggle to talk' (Kirby and Drew, 2003, pp. 134–5).

Also, there are often problems with vowels too, and these may ultimately be the main barrier to progress for speech intelligibility and literacy, especially spelling. There is also frequently a range of associated difficulties (e.g. Stackhouse and Wells, 1997).

Having considered phonetics/articulation, phonology and prosody, it will be apparent that speech difficulties can to some degree be described in terms of these interrelated aspects of speech. For example, speech may be unintelligible because of physical difficulties with articulation (a part of phonetics), and/or difficulties in making meaningful sound contrasts (an aspect of phonology) and/or problems in controlling pitch (an aspect of prosody).

Phonetic difficulties

With articulation problems, the speech difficulties are caused by motor skills being insufficient to produce the sounds for speech. Articulation difficulties may be caused by physical disability if the learning of motor skills necessary for speech is affected. One such physical cause is cleft lip and cleft palate, which can be brought about by genetic factors or by drugs or viruses (such as rubella) in early pregnancy. Cleft lip and cleft palate can be treated surgically. Deterioration in speech skills may also be associated with disabilities such as muscular dystrophy. Cerebral palsy may be associated with neurological effects on oral movements affecting articulation. Also, hearing impairment may cause articulatory difficulties. A congenital malformation of the vocal chord is one cause of 'dysphonia', or difficulty with voicing so that there is no voice or the voice is croaky. This can sometimes be caused by abnormalities in the structure of the larynx. Other causes include paralysis of the vocal chords as a result of accident and genetic factors related to some syndromes.

Prosodic difficulties

Prosodic difficulties concern features of speech such as volume, patterns of intonation and changes in pitch, rhythm and fluency. A child having difficulties with prosody may also have difficulties with the use of language (pragmatics).

Stammering is sometimes considered separately from prosodic difficulties and is a difficulty with fluency, which can make it more difficult for a listener to fully understand what is being said. Where stammering is evident, it is considered advisable to refer the child for assessment by a SALT at an early age. In older pupils, stammering may be related to social and emotional factors and, again, pupils may be referred to a SALT.

Phonological difficulties

With phonological difficulties, there may be no obvious cause of unintelligibility and a restricted speech sound system. However, in some way, the child's development of the use of speech sound to convey meaning will have become individualistic rather than shared and common with others. This may allow those who know the child well to be able to understand much of what he wants to convey but makes it difficult for people who are not familiar with the child to interpret what is said. The child's profile may be specific or delayed or may be a mixture of the two. Delayed and specific profiles are managed differently.

Identification and assessment

Liaison between the teacher, the SENCO and the SALT

Speech difficulties may be noticed or suspected by the teacher when considering the child's development compared with other children of the same age in terms of such guidelines as the National Curriculum 'speaking and listening' expectations. For example, at Key Stage 1, the knowledge, skills and understanding of speaking required includes that:

To speak clearly, fluently and confidently to different people, pupils should be taught to:
a) *speak with clear diction and appropriate intonation*
b) choose words with precision . . . .

(DfEE, 1999a, p. 44, italics added)

At Key Stage 2, in speaking and listening, the knowledge, skills and understanding required includes that:

To speak with confidence in a range of contexts, adapting their speech for a range of purposes and audiences, pupils should be taught to:
a) use vocabulary and syntax that enables them to communicate more complex meanings
  . . .
e) *speak audibly and clearly*, using spoken standard English in formal contexts
f) evaluate their speech and reflect on how it varies.

(DfEE, 1999a, p. 50, italics added)

At Key Stages 3 and 4, in speaking and listening, the knowledge, skills and understanding required includes that:

To speak fluently and appropriately in different contexts, adapting their talk for a range of purposes and audiences, including the more formal, pupils should be taught to:
  . . .
c) use gesture, tone, pace and rhetorical devices for emphasis . . .
  . . .
f) use standard spoken English *fluently* in different contexts.

(DfEE, 1999b, p. 46, italics added)

Naturally, these guidelines are not standardised tests of speech development, nor can they always be regarded as hierarchical or sequential. However, such expectations and the teacher's own experience about the usual development of children's speech will give an indication of possible areas of concern.

The teacher can at any time discuss a concern with the school's SENCO, who will have a whole school overview of pupils with SEN, including pupils with speech and communication difficulties. The SENCO may suggest keeping the child's progress under review or something rather more formal, such as making further more specific assessments and finding out if parents have any concerns or questions about the child's speech development. At some point, the advice of a SALT may be sought who may decide to carry out specialist assessments and observations.

Screening procedures and other assessments

The teacher or others may use some form of screening procedure to check children's attainment and progress. One example is the checklist developed for use with pupils aged 6 to 10 years old by the Association For All Speech Impaired Children (AFASIC, 1991). Among items having relevance to speech are, for example:

◆ omits the beginnings and endings of words e.g. 'pretending' becomes 'tending';
◆ speaks less intelligibly when attempting a lengthy utterance;
◆ shows confusion between voiced and unvoiced sounds.

Such items are ticked if they describe the child. Sections are scored and the scores totalled to give an indication of the child's difficulties.

The following are examples of tests of language development that aim to assess various aspects of language including ones concerning speech.

◆ *Test of Language Development – Primary Third Edition* (*TOLD-P:3*) (Newcomer and Hammill, 1997)

TOLD-P:3 is for pupils aged 4 to 8 years and measures components of spoken language. The child's understanding and meaningful use of words is assessed by the subtests of picture vocabulary, relational vocabulary and oral vocabulary. The subtests of 'grammatic' understanding, sentence imitation and 'grammatic' completion assess different aspects of grammar. Finally, subtests of word articulation, word discrimination and phonemic analysis assess the child's ability to say words correctly and to distinguish words that sound similar.

◆ *Test of Language Development – Intermediate, Third Edition* (*TOLD-I:3*) (Hammill and Newcomer, 1997)

TOLD-I:3 is intended for pupils aged 8 to 12 years and comprises five subtests. Generals, malapropisms and picture vocabulary assess the understanding and meaningful use of words. Aspects of grammar are assessed by the subtests of sentence combining, word ordering and grammatic comprehension.

◆ *Test of Adolescent and Adult Language, Third Edition* (*TOAL-3*) (Hammill et al., 1994)

This test for children aged 12 years to adults aged 24 years assesses aspects of reading, listening, speaking, writing, vocabulary, grammar and receptive and expressive language.

Tests of phonological awareness include:

◆ *Preschool and Primary Inventory of Phonological Awareness* (*PIPA*) (Dodd et al., 2000)

PIPA, which is an individually administered test with UK norms, aims to assess the phonological awareness development of children aged 3 to 6 years 11 months. Six subtests (three for young children) cover: syllable segmentation, rhyme awareness, alliteration awareness, phoneme segmentation, letter knowledge and phoneme isolation.

Assessments in different language contexts

A speech sound can be assessed in isolation, in a syllable, in a word or in connected, perhaps conversational, speech.

Assessing a speech sound in isolation appears at first to have the advantage of singling out the articulation of the sound for particular attention and enabling the assessor to consider if there are difficulties making it. However, some children will be able to make the individual speech sound but be unable to make the sound in a word. The child may be able to make the sound 'b' but be unable to incorporate it in words such as 'big', 'rib' and 'robber'. Assessments of isolated speech sounds sometimes measure the speed and accuracy of the child's articulation, which can indicate whether the child has difficulties with the co-ordination of speech muscles.

When assessing a speech sound in a syllable, speech assessments may use single-syllable words in which the sound to be assessed is the initial or the final sound and the sound being assessed is little influenced by the other sounds of the syllable.

Assessing a speech sound in a word, perhaps by asking the child to name a picture, may be more natural than assessing it in isolation, but other speech sounds in the word can influence the target one. It is therefore important that words and the position of the focus speech sound within it are chosen with care.

One structure for assessing speech sounds is that suggested by Thompson (2003, pp. 15–19). A series of pictures or photographs is used to elicit various speech sounds in initial, final and medial positions in words. For example, a picture of a 'bus' elicits the sound 'b' in its initial position, 'rabbit' gives a 'b' sound in its medial position and 'web' elicits a final 'b' sound. A recording sheet allows the sounds to be noted as being correct or incorrect. The assessment should be conducted one-to-one in quiet surroundings without distractions. The selected speech sounds are based on the phonetic sound rather than the way the word is spelled and the sounds are presented in their single form rather than as a consonant blend (p. 19). If the child is making many errors and speech is unintelligible, advice should be sought from a SALT.

If speech sounds are assessed as they occur in connected speech, this has the advantage of being more natural. But, as with speech sounds in words, the sound of particular interest can be influenced by the other sounds in the words used. Where the child is speaking conversationally, for example about something that interests him, the speech will need to be carefully analysed. The conversation (and other assessments of sounds, words and syllables) may be recorded so that they can be analysed later. Recordings can be made of conversation in different contexts including the child's home, giving the opportunity for the parents, the teacher and the SALT to pool information and co-ordinate their approach.

Distinguishing between speech difficulties and grammar difficulties

It is important that speech difficulties are distinguished in assessments from difficulties with grammar. For example, a speech difficulty involving the sound 's' may make it hard for the child to indicate grammatical features such as plural endings ('coat', 'coats') even if the child knows them. But other children may similarly tend not to indicate such endings even though they are able to make the necessary sound 's'. The difficulty then may be that they do not understand the grammatical convention.

Interventions

A range of interventions are considered in this section that are intended to improve speech, or, as with the subsection, 'Communicating through methods other than speech', provide an alternative means of communication. As speech improves because of successful interventions, it may become apparent that the pupil has other difficulties, for example to do with grammar, that have previously been masked by the speech problems.

Speech and language therapist advice and intervention

As already indicated in the section on identification and assessment, it is open to the SENCO and others to contact the SALT with concerns. It is, of course, important to have a filtering system (which is in effect what aspects of the *Code of Practice* lead to) so that pupils are not referred to a SALT when they have difficulties that it is within the capacity of the school to deal with.

For example, a pupil considered to have DVD may require the intervention of a SALT over a prolonged period to develop the necessary speech patterns and make them automatic (e.g. Kirby and Drew, 2003, p. 135). The SALT is likely to work with other colleagues in a multi-disciplinary approach (e.g. Ripley *et al.*, 2001).

Raising phonological awareness

An approach that lends itself to both whole-class and small-group teaching and that is interesting for all pupils, including those with speech difficulties, is that of raising phonological awareness. Where new vocabulary is introduced, the teacher will encourage a keen interest in the word or phrase. She will clearly teach (and check the pupils' understanding of) various aspects of the vocabulary. These aspects include:

◆ Semantic – what does the word mean? Does it have interesting origins?
◆ Phonological – how do the sounds of the word break up and blend back together? Do the pupils know any similar-sounding words? What are the syllables of the word (younger pupils may enjoy clapping them out)?
◆ Grammatical – how is the word used in sentences?

This can routinely and fairly briefly be accomplished, for example when key words are introduced at the beginning of a lesson. Such an approach is used effectively in both primary and secondary schools and other subject specialists as well as English teachers can use the method to reinforce new vocabulary. An approach using interest in speech sounds is 'Metaphon' (Howell and Dean, 1994). The Metaphon Resource Pack (Dean *et al.*, 1990) is an assessment programme for confirming the identification of suspected phonological disorders and for helping to develop knowledge of sounds and organisation of sound processes. It used with children aged 3 years 6 months to 7 years.

'Soundaround' (Burnett and Wylie, 2002) is a development and curriculum-linked programme for early-years pupils but also for pupils up to Key Stage 1 (5–7 years) and Key Stage 2 (7–11 years). It focuses on sounds first and is intended to help prepare for literacy work.

Playing with Sounds (www.standards.dfes.gov.uk/primary/publications/literacy/948809) (DfES, 2004), a publication intended for Foundation Stage practitioners and Key Stage 1 teachers, includes suggestions for working with pupils in the Foundation Stage and in year 1 on the stepping-stones and early learning goals relating to phonics and the year 1 and year 2 phonics and spelling objectives from the National Literacy Strategy 'Framework for Teaching'.

Error analysis and articulation exercises

The view of speech development that underpins error analysis is one with which some educators and SALTs do not feel entirely comfortable. The child is thought progressively to develop sounds that become increasingly like those made by adults, and where there is a difficulty with speech this is regarded as the child having, as it were, selected the wrong sound, hence the term 'error' analysis. It follows from this that the appropriate intervention is to teach the child the correct sound. For example, if a child tends to pronounce words like 'yes' and 'mess' as 'yeth' and 'meth' (and given that this does not appear to be a phonological difficulty), the approach would indicate enabling the child to recognise the sound that she is making and the distinction between it and the target sound. Articulation exercises would then be carried out to develop and encourage the required sound.

Among the reservations about this approach is that it can suggest that speech sounds are somewhat isolated from the meaning of language. It seems to indicate that speech sounds develop individually rather than within a complex context of the child trying to convey meaning and cultural and media influences. An alternative view is that the motivation for the child to be increasingly precise in making speech sounds is the desire to be understood. Encouraging that motivation is therefore important in the child developing increasingly precise speech sounds. However, the continuing use of the remediating speech sounds approach suggests that there is some attraction in the direct link between identifying what is interpreted as an error and working directly to correct it.

The interventions may include breathing, swallowing and articulation exercises. For example, Thompson (2003, pp. 24–8) suggests activities to increase the child's 'awareness of the speech mechanisms and developing control over tongue, lips, palate and breathing' (p. 24). Such approaches may raise awareness and provide improvement in important underlying muscular control. These activities include to 'encourage the child to lick all the way round the lips. Model the movements so the child can imitate' and 'blow bubbles using a wand and soapy liquid'. With regard to teaching specific sounds, a progressive approach (Thompson, 2003, pp. 37–9) is suggested of:

◆ teaching each sound in isolation (e.g. 'p');
◆ using the sound in nonsense syllables (e.g. 'pah', 'pay', 'pow');

- using the sound in an initial position (in a simple c-v-c word such as 'pig');
- introducing the sound in a final word position (in a simple c-v-c word such as 'cap');
- teaching the sound in a medial position (e.g. 'stopping');
- moving to initial consonant blends (e.g. 'spoon').

Individual task-based programmes

Individual task-based programmes may be developed jointly by the SALT and the teacher. Such programmes take a psycholinguistic perspective focusing on cognitive and linguistic processing.

If, at some point, cognitive and linguistic processing fails, this leads to speech difficulties. Stackhouse and Wells (1997) set out a model of speech processing. They suggest that the brain:

- *receives* speech 'input' through auditory perception;
- *stores* word information in representations of phonological knowledge and awareness (this includes information about the speech sound sequences);
- *accesses* and retrieves knowledge of phonological representations;
- *transforms* this knowledge into motor patterns that produce 'outputs' of speech articulation (or writing).

If this model is adopted, the assessment of a child's difficulties can be identified at particular levels. For example, the pupil may have a difficulty at the level of receiving and recognising speech input because he had a problem with auditory discrimination. There would be medical checks to ensure that the child did not have a hearing impairment. It may be judged that, once the auditory discrimination is secure, the pupil does not appear to have further difficulties with storing word information or accessing and retrieving knowledge of phonological representations or transforming this knowledge into speech. The focus for intervention would therefore be on improving auditory discrimination. At the same time, because the levels are interrelated, work would continue at other levels too, but the particular focus would be auditory discrimination. The task-based programme in such an instance might include a series of activities in which the pupil listens to (perhaps recorded) sounds that are obviously different, then gradually become more similar, to encourage careful attention to sounds and help the child improve auditory discrimination.

Communicating through methods other than speech

For some children with severe speech difficulties, communication may be achieved through non-speech methods such as signing, symbols and computer-aided communication.

A sign language is a system of communication that uses bodily signs: hand and finger movements, facial expressions and body movements. Among signing methods is the Paget–Gorman sign system, which is designed to parallel as closely as possible the grammar (morphology and syntax) of spoken English. It is intended to complement speech and to enhance the ability to write grammatically correctly. (For a brief description of other sign systems, see Farrell, 2003 pp. 149–51.)

Symbols are used as a form of graphical communication, with each symbol representing a concept such as an object, person, activity or attribute. Among the uses of graphic symbols is as communication tools for pupils with speech difficulties. Pupils using alternative or augmentative communication systems use symbols as part of their repertoire. Communication 'grids' in which several symbols are set out in a specified order can enable a pupil to participate in a group session; for example, to support the retelling of a story. A sequence of symbols can be used to indicate a sequence of activities, including a school timetable for a pupil. Communication books can include photographs, symbols and words, so that, for example, a pupil can find a symbol and show the particular page to someone who may not know the symbol, so that they can see the word that is intended. Among commercially available symbols sets are Widgit Rebus and Makaton symbols (see address list). Care is needed to ensure that the pupil makes the link between the real and intended object, activity or person and the symbol, as, although some symbols may seem obvious, they may not be to a child. Indeed, some symbols are not immediately obvious at all.

Information and communication technology, using symbols, allows a large number of symbols to be used flexibly. There are symbol e-mail programmes, and web sites that use symbols. Computer-aided communication may involve the pupil having a voice production device with a computer-based bank of words and sentences that can be produced by pressing the keyboard keys.

Medical/surgical interventions

In relation to speech difficulties, the teacher needs to be aware of medical interventions that have occurred, that are ongoing and that are proposed, because of the impact that these can have on the progress and achievement of the pupil. Surgery may be used, for instance, for cleft lip and cleft palate and chronic middle ear infections. Medication, such as antibiotics, may be prescribed for persistent colds and ear infections.

Behavioural, emotional and social difficulties associated with severe speech difficulties

Children with severe speech difficulties finding it difficult to communicate may become very frustrated. They may be reluctant to communicate or may refuse to try to do so. If required to communicate, they may show signs of intense stress or anxiety. The child may have low self-esteem and may feel rejected by peers (and may in fact be rejected by some). In such circumstances, it is not difficult to recognise that, without support, the child may develop behavioural, emotional and social difficulties. This appears to be supported by evidence of communication problems among populations such as children in care and pupils in schools for children with behavioural, emotional and social difficulties.

An important part of educating pupils with severe speech difficulties is, therefore, to recognise that the pupil may be subject to these pressures and may feel of little worth. The teacher, the SALT and others in the school should work closely with the pupil's family to ensure that the pupil is well supported emotionally and socially. Particular care needs to be taken that the pupils' difficulties with speech are not taken to indicate a general difficulty with learning. Should the teacher make this mistake, there is a danger of her having too-low aspirations of the child's progress. If other pupils are allowed to make this assumption, then their interactions with the pupil may similarly encourage lower expectations. Such low aspirations can further hinder the pupil's progress and willingness to learn. Also, direct efforts to help the pupil communicate intelligibly are likely to improve the pupil's skills and self-esteem.

Children for whom English is an additional language

Children for whom English is an additional language and who are experiencing speech difficulties may manifest difficulties in one language or both and will require assessing in both languages before appropriate strategies can be determined.

THINKING POINTS

Readers may wish to consider:

◆ continuing to develop an understanding of speech and the interventions that are used for speech difficulties;
◆ using such understanding so that work with a SALT where this is indicated is more intelligible and meaningful educationally;
◆ the times at which direct intervention by a SALT may be necessary and when it may be beneficial for a teacher or teaching assistant to be involved in a programme developed by a SALT, perhaps involving developing related goals in IEPs, in planning for literacy work, in topics and so on.

KEY TEXT

Martin, D. (2000) *Teaching Children with Speech and Language Difficulties*, London, David Fulton Publishers.

This book includes chapters covering assessment (Chapter 4), classroom approaches (Chapter 5) and whole-school strategies (Chapter 6).

Chapter 3

Difficulties with grammar

INTRODUCTION

In considering the nature of grammar, this chapter distinguishes 'syntax' and 'morphology', both of which are explained. I consider difficulties in the development of grammar. The chapter looks at the identification and assessment of difficulties with grammar with reference to: National Curriculum expectations; screening and standardised assessment; liaison between the teacher, the SENCO and the SALT; assessment and monitoring through descriptive grammar; and calculating a child's mean length utterance.

Interventions and their rationale are explained. These include: direct, clear, understandable communication by the teacher; extra time and over-learning for the pupil; planned opportunities for group discussion; using visual and auditory aids to support communication; and encouraging a whole-class interest in word order and grammatical features of language. Also considered are planned opportunities for the child to use words and structures with which he is having difficulty; modelling (and shaping) of pupils' responses; and supporting the development of grammatical utterances by writing and reading activities.

Grammar and its development

What is grammar?

Grammar concerns the rules for putting words together to make sentences. The term 'syntax' is sometimes used as a synonym for 'grammar', although grammar can be understood as including 'syntax' and 'morphology', as will be explained later. While one might at first think of the written form of words when considering grammar, in spoken utterances, as well as in the written form, grammar relates to the way words are put together in sequences.

In sentences, some words (phrases) that are particularly closely grammatically related are said to form 'constituents' of the sentence and can often be replaced by a single alternative word. These are the words that were parsed in traditional grammar lessons into such constituents as: noun phrases, verb phrases, prepositional phrases, adverbial phrases and so on. For example, consider the sentence below:

Dr Grant had seen the dinosaurs.
He   had seen them.
NP   VP   NP

It will be seen that the constituents, 'Dr Grant', 'had seen' and 'the dinosaurs' can be identified as noun phrase (NP), verb phrase (VP) and noun phrase (NP) respectively and that single words can be substituted for some of the constituents ('He' for 'Dr Grant' and 'them' for 'the dinosaurs').

Among the rules for combining words are ones at the constituent level, phrase level and word level.

♦   At the constituent level, making meaning in utterances is structured by the patterns in which combinations of words are placed, such as NP and VP and word order.
♦   The phrase level involves, for example, function words such as 'the' in the sentence, '*The* sun is shining', or 'but' in the sentence, 'I went to the shop *but* it was closed.'
♦   At the word level, making meaning is structured by inflections (e.g. word endings) and by function words such as 'by', 'with' and 'of', which can be used to indicate a meaning relationship.

Another related way of considering grammar is in terms of:

♦   syntax, which refers to the rules for making words into sentences;
♦   morphology, that is, grammatical changes to particular words.

Clearly, to develop age-appropriate grammar, children need a good vocabulary and, therefore, a child with poor vocabulary will require help developing this too. It is also important to develop function words. The distinctions and ways of looking at grammar that have been introduced above are useful in describing typical grammar and difficulties with grammar.

The development of grammar

When, in early language development, children begin to join words together in two-word utterances, this is taken to be the beginnings of the child's awareness that words have a grammatical meaning, that is, that putting words together has meaning.

Typically, children's development can be adequately described as moving from one-word to four-word utterances until, at about the age of 3 years, they begin to use complex utterances with several clauses and phrases. Utterances begin to manifest the development of combinations of the grammatical features that were described earlier: constituents, phrases, inflections and function words. Beyond the four-word stage, describing or analysing utterances in terms of word count becomes less and less satisfactory because so much of grammatical meaning is missed by such an approach, as utterances increase in complexity. It is more fruitful to analyse the relationships of the grammatical constituents (NP, VP, AP) and the development of phrase level structure.

Typically, children's grammar shows development at different levels: constituent, phrase, inflection and function word level. For pupils with grammatical difficulties, their utterances may indicate development at the constituent level but less development at the phrase level (function word, adjective etc.) and word level (inflections). Consequently, although the utterances tend to comprise the main information-carrying words, they sound rather stilted.

Compound utterances develop as children become able to grammatically connect two ideas because they are related. For example, the ideas may be related because they are similar or different or because one follows on from the other ('She was bored *so* she went to the theme park'). Other compound utterances involve embedding one sentence in another ('I like the coat *that* I bought last summer').

As constituent and phrase level grammar develops, so does morphemic grammar affecting word level relationships in utterances (words, function words and inflections). Morphemes may be 'free' or 'bound'. Free morphemes are single words (e.g. 'dog', 'give') or function words (e.g. 'the', 'under'). Bound morphemes are inflections attached to words ('-ly' as in 'happ*ily*' or '-ing' as in 'swimm*ing*'). Typically, many children have acquired many early emerging morphemes (including '-ing', '-ed', 'a', 'the') by the age of two and a half years (Wells, 1985).

Difficulties with grammar: possible causal factors

Among factors implicated in grammatical difficulties in spoken language are genetic, neurological and physical ones. For example, for a small group of children, there may be a hereditary predisposition as indicated by the prevalence of language difficulties in other members of the family, particularly in the male line. Neurological weakness, for example that brought about by birth trauma, appears to be implicated in the case of language difficulties in some children. Also, physical damage to the brain through accidents or viral infections may lead to severe language difficulties.

Associated with language difficulties are poverty and hearing impairment. Where these factors are implicated, they are considered the primary difficulty and language difficulties are a concomitant of them, being therefore secondary. This does not imply of course that poverty is a special educational need in itself or that the language difficulty concerned is less important, but it does suggest that the other factors should be borne in mind.

Some research has suggested strong links between poverty and language delay. In a study published in 2002, of pre-school children from disadvantaged socio-economic backgrounds, over half were considered to experience language delay and language skills were found to be significantly below cognitive abilities (Locke *et al.*, 2002). A child from a disadvantaged socio-economic background is also more likely to suffer illness leading to absences from school and have poorer nutrition than other children, both factors being likely to make learning more difficult.

A child with a hearing impairment may need to be taught sign language. There are grammatical implications for sign languages. British Sign Language (BSL) is an example of a system that has grammatical structure at the constituent and word order levels. The Paget–Gorman system is an instance of a sign language reflecting the phrase and word level grammatical structures of spoken language. Some children with hearing impairment experience additional difficulties in developing grammatical structures. (Sign languages are considered in Chapter 3 of the book, *The Effective Teacher's Guide to Sensory Impairment and Physical Disability: Practical Strategies*, in the present series.)

Difficulties with syntax

A child may show signs of having difficulty with grammatical structures at about the age of 3 years. These may be difficulties with the order of words and with making sentences of four or more words. The child may have difficulties with function words. A child may use telegraphic utterances when they are no longer age appropriate, such as 'me tired' for 'I am tired'. The key words are included but the function words are often missed out in speaking.

Some children can formulate simple sentences but have difficulty making compound sentences. This may be because the child has difficulties with auditory sequential memory and may be unable to handle long word sequences. The child may also have difficulties with the grammatical relationships implicated in connecting the ideas that are complicatedly hierarchical, dependent, embedded or causal (Martin and Miller, 2003, p. 73).

The child may lack the linguistic knowledge of the rules necessary to recognise the grammatical role of words, such as the difference between nouns and verbs. For similar reasons, the child may not be able to recognise the appropriate structures for verbs (Van der Lely, 1994).

There may be a difficulty with short-term memory, which may cause problems formulating sentences; or the child may have difficulty with grammatical structures because these are embedded and hierarchical, leading also to problems formulating sentences. Many children with specific language difficulties experience pervasive memory and organisational problems and require help and support with general organisation.

The child may have processing difficulties related to working memory. The child cannot make sentence structures with familiar words or use a two-noun phrase with a verb because the demands of processing these requirements are too great for the child. Difficulties with grammar are the manifestation of this.

From a broader cognitive perspective, the child may have problems with auditory memory, auditory sequencing, attention and reading and writing. To the extent that they are contributing factors to grammatical development, work may be undertaken to improve them. At the same time, the teacher can help the pupil more directly with the development of grammatical skills.

Although difficulties with syntax (and morphology) are considered from the expressive point of view (the child's utterances), many children with grammatical difficulties have problems with the receptive aspect of grammar; in other words, with understanding grammatical structures that they have not yet acquired expressively.

Difficulties with morphology

As indicated earlier, morphology refers to grammatical structure usually in the form of prefixes and suffixes. This can add grammatical information and change the word class of the word involved. For example, many nouns have plural endings, such as 'cat' and 'cats', while verbs may have different endings, such as 'talk', 'talking' and 'talked'. Usually, many children will have acquired many of these sorts of morphemes by as early as two-and-a-half years (Wells, 1985), if not expressively, then receptively. Children who have difficulties with grammatical structure, however, find morphology hard and may require specific teaching and practice in order to learn it.

More complex aspects of morphology include changes to words that negate the meaning, for example 'stable' and 'unstable' or 'like' and 'dislike'. Suffixes can change the grammatical class to which the original word belongs, as when the adjective 'kind' is changed to the noun 'kindness'. Typically, children begin to work on such examples of morphology between the ages of 10 and 12 years as part of the National Curriculum programmes of study in England.

Identification and assessment of difficulties with grammar

Bishop summarises some of the subtlety and complexities of grammar:

> When words are put together, the whole is far greater than the sum of its parts. By combining words one can generate an enormously complex range of meanings. Verbs provide a means for expressing relationships between entities; who did what to whom, who experienced what, how an object was acted upon, and so on. Adverbs and adjectives enable one to describe qualities of actions, events or objects. But this is not all. Our powers of expression are enormously increased by the use of linguistic terms that function solely to modify meanings of content words. Some of these are 'function words', such as 'but', 'not', 'in', or 'from', which express logical, spatial and temporal relationships. Others are grammatical inflexions, which cannot stand alone, and are always appended to a content word, such as plural, '-s', past tense '-ed', or comparative '-er'. Both uninflected words and inflexions are morphemes, i.e. minimal units of meaning. Morphemes that cannot stand on their own are known as bound morphemes, and those that can do so are free morphemes. Meaning is expressed not just by morphemes that are present in a sentence, but by the order in which they occur.
>
> (1997, p. 116)

With such complexities in mind, one cannot be over-rigid in applying a notion or framework of typical development to underpin the identification and assessment of difficulties with grammar. It is well to remember that there is variation in development and the pace of development that is considered statistically normal and occurs in children without necessarily indicating the existence of difficulties. At the same time, the teacher will be aware of the importance of early intervention, which implies not treating possible early indications of difficulty too cautiously. There is clearly a tension between these two positions requiring careful professional judgement supplemented as necessary by advice from other colleagues. Related to this is the difficulty of knowing with much certainty whether the apparent difficulties are going to prove temporary or chronic.

National Curriculum expectations

At Key Stage 1 of the National Curriculum for speaking and listening, pupils should be taught to 'choose words with precision' and '*organise* what they say' (DfEE/QCA, 1999a, p. 44, italics added). At Key Stage 2, they should be taught to 'use vocabulary and *syntax* that enables them to communicate more complex meanings' and 'speak audibly and clearly, using *spoken Standard English* in formal contexts' (p. 50, italics added). At Key Stages 3 and 4, pupils should be taught to 'vary word choices, including technical vocabulary, and *sentence structure* for different audiences' (DfEE/QCA, 1999b, p. 46, italics added). These expectations of grammar will give some indication to the teacher of what constitutes the expectations of typical pupils and when a pupil might be having difficulties, compared with others.

Screening and standardised assessment

Screening tests routinely used by the school may suggest that a child is experiencing difficulties with grammar. An example of such a screening device is the checklists published by the Association For All Speech Impaired Children (AFASIC, 1991), which have already been mentioned in relation to speech in Chapter 2: 'Difficulties with speech'. In relation to difficulties with grammar, the checklist includes such items as 'offers limited verbal comments on own activities'. An example of a specific assessment for syntax is the *South Tyneside Assessment of Syntactic Structures* (*STASS*) (Armstrong and Ainley, 1988).

Other assessments include the following.

◆ *The Reynell Developmental Language Scales III* (Edwards *et al.*, 1997)

These scales are used by SALTs to assess children suspected of experiencing language problems. There is an expressive scale and a comprehension scale, which concentrate on the structural aspects of language and how they influence the acquisition and use of language.

◆ *The Wilson Syntax Screening Test* (Wilson, 2000)

This assessment, for children aged 4 years to 5 years 11 months, is for use by teachers, SENCOs and SALTs. It comprises a 20-item screening test, which assesses the ability of the child to produce grammatical constructions that are known to be problematic for children with specific language difficulty.

◆ *Test of Word and Grammatical Awareness* (Shaw, 2000)

For use by speech and language therapists, educational psychologists and specialist teachers, this assessment measures a child's awareness of words and grammar. It is used with children aged 4 years 6 months to 8 years and takes approximately 20 minutes to administer.

◆ *Derbyshire Language Scheme* (Knowles and Masidlover, 1982)

The Derbyshire Language Scheme (www.derbyshire-language-scheme.co.uk) is an intervention programme that includes assessment materials allowing the SALT or teacher to establish a pupil's current levels of skill and indicating teaching activities aimed to develop them.

◆ *Assessment of Comprehension and Expression 6–11* (Adams *et al.*, 2001)

For use with children aged 6 years to 11 years 11 months, this assessment aims to identify children who have delays with or impairments to their comprehension or expression of language and includes coverage of syntactic formulation.

◆ *Language Assessment, Remediation and Screening Procedure* (*LARSP*) (Crystal, 1976)

This provides a linguistic analysis of utterances and is usually used by SALTs or by teachers in liaison with SALTs.

Liaison between the teacher, the SENCO and the SALT or educational psychologist

Initial investigation may include checking the child's level of understanding of plurals, tenses, negatives, prepositions, pronouns and questions. Assessment pictures can be used. For example, for plurals, there might be a picture of one cat and a picture of several cats and the child would be asked to 'Show me the cat' or 'Show me the cats'. To assess understanding negatives, the pictures might show 'sitting' and 'not sitting' (e.g. standing). For prepositions, pictures can show an item 'behind' or 'in front of' another item or one item can be shown 'inside' a container (Thompson, 2003, pp. 51–4). As well as pictures, objects can be used so long as what is conveyed is clear. Preliminary observation may suggest that a child could have difficulties with grammar, but ongoing observation is important to monitor progress or lack of it over a period of time.

Where the teacher has a concern about a pupil's development of grammar, she is likely to observe the child for a period of time to check if impressions appear to be reasonably well founded. She will then speak initially with the SENCO, who may make further observations. The SENCO may at some point consider seeking the advice of the SALT or the educational psychologist, representing involvement at the Early Years Action or School Action aspect of the *Special Educational Needs Code of Practice* (DfES, 2001) graduated response. Ongoing observation and monitoring by the teacher is still relevant when the SALT has been involved.

Assessment and monitoring through descriptive grammar

Descriptive grammar concerns the grammar that is used by people in their spoken language. It describes the rules that exist in the speaker's use of language and any variations from the rules, but carries no notions of correct or incorrect grammar from some imaginary point outside what real speakers say and how they say it.

As such, descriptive grammar can indicate the development of a child's grammar at different points in time, including as it approaches the way that adults usually use grammar. The descriptions can indicate the skills a child has already acquired without necessarily overemphasising the features that are not developed.

Mean length of utterance

Analysing a sample of the child's spontaneous language and counting the number of morphemes in each of a number of utterances can assess an aspect of grammatical development. For example, in the utterance, 'I eat-ed a cake', there are five morphemes. The number of morphemes used in each of the utterances is averaged to give the mean length of utterance (MLU). Typical MLUs for children of different ages are used for comparison. For example, typically, a child uses two morphemes by the age of 24 months, and four morphemes by the time he is about 40 months old. Bishop (1997, p. 92) suggests that the MLU is a popular index of grammatical complexity because it is easy to compute and that, in normally developing children, there is a fairly linear relationship between the MLU and the child's chronological age.

Interventions

Direct, clear and understandable teacher communication

Ensuring the attention of the pupil is a precursor to the pupil being able to benefit from the effective communication of the teacher. If a pupil has difficulty interpreting the grammatical structure and meaning of utterances, it is important that the teacher communicates effectively with the pupil in order to maintain the pupil's attention. This will involve using shorter utterances. Also essential is to check that communication is understood; this can be achieved through questioning the pupil, and through the pupil making a previously agreed signal to alert the teacher if there is something that he does not understand.

Extra time and over-learning

A pupil experiencing difficulties with morphology may benefit from being given extra time to develop a clearer understanding of the 'rules' involved, being given more examples and being given the opportunity to over-learn some of them through repetition. This may involve some pre-tutoring in preparation for a lesson, the help of a learning support assistant (LSA) during a lesson to reinforce points, or some post-lesson tutoring to check and develop understanding. The aim is to develop a pupil's confidence and improve his skills without making him bored by any necessary rote or drill learning. Such rote learning should be kept brief and made as interesting as possible for younger children, perhaps being presented in the form of games.

Planned opportunities for group discussion

When organising group discussions that will include a pupil or pupils with difficulties with grammar, the teacher will need to be careful that their grammatical development is encouraged. This will be helped, for example, where the pupil has had support with the structures likely to be used in the discussion (perhaps a short practice talk with an LSA. The pre-teaching or preparation can include some of the grammatical structures likely to be used with the relevant vocabulary. For example, if the discussion is to involve explaining a procedure, then linking words such as 'next', 'then' or 'after that' would be practised. Should the discussion involve events in the distant past, expressions such as 'in the twelfth century' or 'two hundred years ago' might be practised, as appropriate, to ensure that the pupil understands their grammatical use.

This type of brief practice will tend to raise the pupil's confidence, enable him to participate in the discussion and, because it quickly links with a meaningful situation (the subsequent discussion), will tend to be motivating.

Using visual and auditory aids to support communication

To the extent that difficulty with grammar reflects a difficulty with sequencing and ordering and a lack of understanding as to how such features as word order change meaning, using sequencing instructions is likely to help the pupil. A series of picture cards indicating the steps of a process or set of instructions is an example. The teacher may, when necessary, occasionally pre-record instructions on an audiotape recorder or compact disc recorder so that a pupil having difficulties with grammar can, if he wishes, hear brief instructions several times, perhaps over headphones to avoid distracting other pupils. This would, of course, have to be built into the lesson at a suitable time so that the pupil is not missing other aspects of the lesson that are also important.

Planned opportunities for the child to use words and structures with which he is having difficulty

One approach to difficulties with syntax is to use the ability that the child has in understanding meaning to help him develop strategies based on meaning. The teacher would work closely with the SALT, who would identify the grammatical function words and structures with which the child is having difficulty. Using these words and structures as meaningful units can be built into the child's other work and, if the child is writing, it can be built into written work too. This provides a context for the development of grammar, rather than drills that may not be as motivating or understandable.

Modelling (and shaping) of pupils' responses

Modelling and shaping are both behavioural interventions. Modelling involves providing the pupil with an example of the accepted way to perform a task, while shaping involves encouraging the pupil to behave ever closer to the desired standard. In the present context, using modelling, without appearing to correct everything the pupil having difficulties with grammar utters, the teacher can model to the pupil the grammatical forms of utterances and praise and encourage the pupil when he copies or spontaneously uses such forms correctly. Role-play can be used to model suitable grammar and the pupil can thereby practise correct forms.

Shaping grammar involves rewarding, usually through praise, approximations of the correct grammatical form. The opportunity to develop skills in this way in small discussion groups can be particularly helpful for pupils experiencing difficulties with grammar.

Encouraging an interest in word order and grammatical features by whole class

An interest in the grammar of spoken utterances can be encouraged for the whole class by emphasising the importance of word order or morphology, as appropriate. In English, this may involve listening to and talking about audiotaped or video-taped conversation, speeches and discussions (not necessarily of the children themselves) and focusing on grammar. In other subjects of the curriculum, it will be appropriate from time to time to point out distinctive aspects of the grammar of utterances. In history, a series of phrases about time may be used in a writing frame ('Two hundred years ago,' 'It was only two hundred years ago that'). Grammar games and activities can make a contribution to this by motivating pupils and, ideally, making learning fun.

Supporting grammatical utterances by writing and reading activities

In the same vein as encouraging the interest of the whole class in the grammar of spoken utterances, a similar interest should be routinely encouraged through writing and reading. The literacy hour of course makes provision for this in primary schools, and in secondary schools the beginning of lessons in many subjects can, as appropriate, include a reference to relevant grammar. For example, in a science lesson, the teacher may remind the pupils of the formal grammatical passive structure of reporting in experiments, perhaps providing a model sentence or two of writing. In reading too, the structure of sentences and morphology will sometimes be usefully picked out as of interest. In design and technology (food), where written instructions in the form of recipes are followed, the teacher can point out the structure of these in using direct, short sentences or phrases to ensure clarity. Such examples will indeed help pupils to write their own recipes or write instructions in relation to other subjects. History lessons involving the examination of old documents will draw attention to the grammar of other times. In fiction, the manipulation of grammar to create particular effects can be noted.

Derbyshire Language Scheme activities

The *Derbyshire Language Scheme* (Knowles and Masidlover, 1982) (www.derbyshire-language-scheme.co.uk), mentioned in the earlier section concerning assessment, is an intervention programme targeting early language skills. It is structured, with graded objectives beginning from single words and moving on to long, complex sentences. Assessment materials allow the SALT and the teacher to establish a child's current skill levels.

THINKING POINTS

Readers may wish to consider with reference to a particular school:

◆ the extent to which existing approaches to speech and language development are likely to enhance a child's development of grammar;
◆ the effectiveness of existing ways of identifying and assessing difficulties with grammar and the effectiveness of steps taken to help the child;
◆ what more could be done to improve existing provision.

KEY TEXTS

Bishop, D. V. M. (1997) *Uncommon Understanding: Development and Disorders of Language Comprehension in Children*, Hove, Psychology Press.

Chapter 5, 'Grammatical knowledge in sentence comprehension', examines grammar, as the chapter title indicates, in relation to comprehension. It outlines some of the theories of how grammar develops, including that of the Universal Grammar proposed by Chomsky.

Martin, D. and Miller, C. (2003) *Speech and Language Difficulties in the Classroom*, London, David Fulton Publishers.

The reader might be particularly interested in Chapter 5, 'Difficulties formulating sentences', which concerns syntax and morphology.

Chapter 4

Difficulties with meaning

INTRODUCTION

This chapter considers the development of an understanding of meaning
(semantics) in language. I examine meaning and its development in terms of
what is meant by the term 'meaning' and then discuss labelling, packaging,
networking, idiom, grammatical aspects of meaning, and meaning relations. The
chapter then looks at difficulties in each of these aspects in turn. I consider identification and assessment, focusing on National Curriculum assessments, screening
and testing procedures, liaison between the teacher, the SENCO and the SALT,
vocabulary assessment, and word elicitation tasks for idiom.

The chapter presents various interventions relating to the difficulties children
experience. Improving labelling can be achieved through direct teaching and
structured experience; play and pictures representing objects or actions; the use
of sign systems and graphic symbols; picture matching, printed labels and sign
language for pupils with difficulties storing auditory information; and developing word-finding skills. Helping packaging is done through analysing the
child's perceptions, and by means of exemplars, models and reshaping of the child's
utterances. Networking is assisted through direct teaching in a range of subjects,
using and explaining key polysemic words in subjects, teaching alternatives for
polysemic words, and teaching how grammatical context can change word meaning.
Helping the understanding of idiom is achieved through examples and explanations, and analysing a child's processing. Helping an understanding of grammar
and meaning is achieved through direct teaching. The understanding of meaning
relations is assisted by practice and exemplars, structured experiences and over-
learning.

Meaning and its development

What does 'meaning' mean?

When examining meaning in language, various terms are used to capture the unit
of meaning. For example, the word 'die' and the words 'pass away' can be used

to convey the same meaning; in fact, perhaps because of the reluctance of some contemporary societies to discuss death, it is often observed that there is a wealth of euphemisms for 'death'. Given the fact that a word or several words can be used when intending the same meaning, the term 'lexeme' is often used to indicate the unit of meaning instead of alternatives such as 'word' or 'vocabulary'. This allows the notion of meaning to include meaning being conveyed by the use of one word or several.

It will be apparent that meaning is much more than the use of a lexeme. A word or several words may be used but the speaker may not understand what they mean. For the lexeme to be meaningful, the speaker has to have a certain amount of knowledge of concepts. For example, a child may say the word 'dog', but if she has never seen a dog and if the word is not in someway associated with the concept of dog, then one would not be able to say that the child understood the meaning of the word.

Similarly, to grasp the meaning of lexemes implies that other cognitive factors support the understanding of meaning. The child's memory will need to be able to link the object and the word. Therefore, when the object is next seen, the word will be available, or, when the child next uses the word, it will be with some memory of the concept and object associated with the word.

The context in which the word is used is also an indication that the child has grasped its meaning and is therefore a part of our understanding of meaning. So a child may use a word such as 'cat' in an utterance that bears no apparent relationship to the usual understanding or meaning of the word. If the context does not support the word, then a child cannot normally be said to have understood its meaning.

Aitchison, in *Words in the Mind* (1994, Chapter 6), suggests that, in acquiring meaning, children have three different but related tasks: a labelling task, a packaging task and a network-building task, each of which is explained below.

Labelling

The child 'must discover that a sequence of sounds can be used as names for things' (Aitchison, 1994, p. 87). What seem to be early words are often better regarded as 'ritual accompaniments to a whole situation' (p. 88). Later, a child begins to broaden the circumstances under which he produces the ritual utterances and this leads to what could more securely be seen as labelling and symbolising.

To understand the lexeme as a label is to regard it as a content word referring to an external phenomenon, which may be an object, a person, an action or an attribute. The child interacts with parents from an early age as they encourage the linking of sounds with phenomena so that the child comes to associate the two. It becomes noticeable that the child also, from about the age of 3 years, asks questions about objects and other features of his environment. This process appears to be underpinned by and to necessitate a certain level of maturation and skill development. For example, labelling is facilitated if the child:

◆ is able to direct attention physically and cognitively to an object or event that is being named;

◆ has some notion that objects may disappear from view and reappear but that they continue to exist and are the same object (object permanence);

◆ recognises that objects and events can be symbolised by pictures or other items (e.g. a toy car).

Another important aspect of what it means to be able to label phenomena is 'word-finding', that is, that the child is able to access and retrieve words that connect with a stimulus such as a picture or an item.

Packaging

In the packaging task, children 'must find out which things can be packaged together under one label' (Aitchison, 1994, p. 87).

A lexeme is also understood to include a 'package' of conceptual and grammatical meaning. Conceptual meaning may at first be limited (under-extended), as when a child can label his own dog as 'dog' but would not be able to understand the word and its meaning in connection with other dogs. Concepts are said to be overextended if the word is used with too wide a reference, for example if the word 'dog' was used to refer to all small animals. Suggested explanations for over-extension include that the child lacks knowledge. He may know the word 'duck' and use it for the correct creature but may also use the word for, say, a crow.

Gradually, the child comes to know the parameters of a word. Another view is that the child may work from certain prototypes of phenomena but analyse them differently to adults. For example, the word 'moon' may be used for the correct phenomenon but also for a cow's horn because it is crescent-shaped like a phase of the moon, and for a leaf because it is shiny like the moon.

Grammatical meaning relates to the grammatical role of the word in a sentence that affects its meaning, for example whether grammar conveys an active or passive role for the object 'milk' in 'The cat drank the *milk*' or 'The *milk* was drunk by the cat'.

Network-building

In the network-building task, children 'must work out how words relate to one another' (Aitchison, 1994, p. 87). Networking relates to the fact that the lexeme also gains meaning from its relationship with other words. For example, the relationship may be based on whether a word relates to others because it is a synonym or antonym or whether it is in the same category ('paper' and 'pencil' both being in the category of 'stationery'). Children tend to learn words that happen to be subordinates ('red', 'blue', 'yellow') before learning the superordinate word ('colour'). Word relationships may be based on serial connection (e.g. months of the year).

Among other ways in which words are related is by sounding the same (homonyms), for example 'meet' and 'meat', or by being written in the same way (homographs), for instance 'wind' meaning breeze and 'wind' meaning to wind up a mechanism.

Some words are written and pronounced in the same way but have several meanings (polysemy), for example 'top' meaning variously a spinning toy, the summit or upper part of something, to better someone or something and so on. The correct meaning is usually determined by the child using contextual clues as predictors, so that in a conversation about competition the word 'top' is likely to be used in the sense of bettering someone, rather than to refer to the spinning toy. Similarly, different meanings are usually learned as the polysemic word appears and is taught in different contexts. Some polysemic words have a literal and an abstract meaning, such as 'soft' meaning either not resistant to the touch or over-compliant when referring to a person.

Grammatical context can change the meaning of polysemic words as in phrasal verbs such as 'put' functioning as a preposition ('put on', 'put across', 'put away') (Martin and Miller, 2003, p. 92).

Idiom

An idiom is an expression meaning more than, or something different to, the sum of the individual words comprising it. Such expressions notoriously cause problems for foreigners learning to speak English. For children, such expressions are learned as chunks of meaning. Examples of idiom include proverbs ('a stitch in time saves nine'), sayings ('mustn't grumble') and sequences of words conveying an idea ('take away' for 'subtract'). Developmentally, children under 8 years old prefer to analyse each word or morphological unit in a series of words or utterances to help them with grammatical and lexical information. Older pupils and adults increasingly organise language into word strings and formulaic sequences, perhaps because this results in quicker processing (Nippold and Martin, 1989, cited in Wray, 2001).

Grammatical aspects of meaning

Words can, of course, be described according to the part of speech (or 'word class') they occupy in an utterance: noun, adjective, pronoun and so on. A difficulty with describing words in this way is that the same word can have different grammatical functions, so that 'cat' in the sentence, 'I bought a white cat', is a noun, while in the sentence, 'I closed the cat flap', it is an adjective. As children develop speech, they tend to assign to each word they use a single grammatical function. 'Cat' may always be a noun, 'red' invariably an adjective and so on. Only gradually do children come to learn that the same word can have different grammatical roles.

Meaning relations

A sentence has a meaning structure that can remain the same even though the grammatical structure may change, as when the meaning remains whether a sentence is in the active or passive voice. For example, the sentence, 'Amy told a story' and 'The story was told by Amy' convey the same meaning but have different grammatical structures.

Difficulties with meaning: their nature and causes

Difficulties in learning to label

Children who have difficulties with labelling may not have made links between the spoken word and the object, action or other phenomena. They may not have sufficiently developed their concepts as their experience has been limited.

The child may not have developed the skills and understanding that underpins the understanding of labels, or may not be able to direct attention physically and cognitively to an object or event being labelled, or may lack the notion of object permanence. He may not recognise that objects and events can be symbolised by pictures or other items.

The child may have difficulty storing the auditory information necessary to make the links for labelling.

Sometimes, a child may have developed a sense of symbolising through play and the use of pictures but may still have difficulty with the particular symbolisation relating to learning words, perhaps because of a difficulty making sense of and storing auditory information.

A child may be thought to have word-finding problems, but, before one assumes such a difficulty, one should make sure that it is not the child's comprehension that is the problem and that the child has sufficient understanding of what is being said and that she understands the meaning of the words that are supposedly being sought. Let us assume that all this has been checked and that word-finding difficulties are still indicated. The child may be able to recognise a word, for example 'shoes', so that, if someone says the word, the child could say what shoes are. She may be able to understand the word and be able to explain that shoes are worn on the feet and that there is a left shoe and a right shoe. In spite of all this, the child has difficulty, if shown a shoe or a picture of a shoe, of 'finding' the word in order to be able to say it. Similarly, in general conversation, the child may want to use the word but not be able to 'find' it. It appears that the difficulty is therefore one of access and retrieval. The meaning of a word is not established until there are secure links between the word and the phenomenon to which it refers. A child having difficulties with word-finding may show certain typical behaviours, such as excessive use of expressions that have no meaning but that keep the utterance going (e.g. 'uh', 'ehm'), using stereotyped phrases (e.g. 'sort of', 'kind of') and using filler words (e.g. 'pass me the *thingy*').

Difficulties with packaging

Difficulties with packaging are indicated if a child continues at an age when it is not typical to show under-extended conceptual meaning (e.g. 'dog' refers to only the child's dog) or overextended conceptual meaning (e.g. 'dog' refers to all small animals). Difficulties with the grammatical meaning aspect of packaging relate to problems understanding that the grammatical role of the word in a sentence affects the word's meaning.

Difficulties with networking

Difficulties with networking (the lexeme gaining meaning from its relationship with other words) relating to synonyms may be because of a child's conceptual rigidity – the idea that one word can only mean one thing. A difficulty with antonyms may relate to the difficulty for any child that antonyms can be relative. A mouse is 'small' compared with a 'big' elephant, but 'big' compared with a 'small' ant.

Regarding subordinate and superordinate words, some pupils have difficulties keeping boundaries of similar semantic fields and may include fruits in lists of vegetables and vice versa. Children may have difficulties with word relationships that concern serial connections (e.g. months of the year), but sequencing problems may go well beyond such isolated difficulties. Difficulties with homonyms (for example, 'meet' and 'meat') or homographs (for instance, 'wind' meaning breeze and 'wind' meaning to wind up a mechanism) are likely to emerge in literacy work. Difficulties may arise with polysemy, where words are written and pronounced in the same way but have several meanings (e.g. 'top'). The child has difficulty determining the correct meaning using contextual clues or recognising the abstract meaning of the word. The child may have difficulty grasping that grammatical context can change the meaning of polysemic words, as in phrasal verbs such as 'put' functioning as a preposition ('put on', 'put across', 'put away') (Martin and Miller, 2003, p. 92).

Difficulties with idiom

Difficulties with idiom (an expression meaning more than, or something different to, the sum of the individual words comprising it) arise when children appear not to learn these expressions as chunks of meaning but as literal sequences of individual words. The holistic meaning of the idiom is therefore inaccessible (Wray, 2001).

Difficulties with grammatical aspects of meaning

Most children develop from assigning to each word they use a single grammatical function and come to understand that the same word can have different grammatical roles. Children who have difficulty with meaning in language may have difficulty in recognising that a word whose meaning they thought they understood has a different meaning by virtue of being used in a different grammatical role. The word 'green' is not only an adjective that conveys colour; it is also a noun indicating an area of land.

Difficulties with meaning relations

Some children have difficulties understanding that the meaning structure of a sentence can remain the same, even though its grammatical structure may change, for example from the active to the passive voice. The child would have difficulty changing the grammatical structure while maintaining the meaning, so, in changing the sentence, 'The dog chased the rabbit', to 'The rabbit was chased by the dog', the child would find it hard to retain the meaning. Furthermore, on hearing the two utterances, the child might think that the second utterance meant that the rabbit did the chasing. If a child has sequencing difficulties, for example where the child has DVD, these need to be borne in mind when seeking to assess and remedy difficulties with meaning relations.

Identification and assessment

National Curriculum

In Key Stage 1 of the National Curriculum, pupils should be taught to 'choose words with precision' (DfEE/QCA, 1999a, p. 44), while at Key Stage 2 pupils should be taught to 'use vocabulary and syntax that enables them to communicate more complex meanings' (p. 50). At Key Stages 3 and 4, pupils should be taught to 'vary word choices, including technical vocabulary, and sentence structure for different audiences' (DfEE/QCA, 1999b, p. 46). While such requirements give general indications of what is expected and therefore what is typical of pupils, the teacher's experience of what constitutes typical language development, particularly in relation to the development of meaning, will also be important.

Testing procedures

Some tests use a 'confrontation naming approach', in which the person assessing the child points to a picture, object or activity and asks the child to name it. It depends on the child being able to understand that, for example, a picture represents something and being able to recognise what that 'something' is. It is sometimes criticised for not providing the context (and therefore the contextual clues) in which the word would normally be used and consequently perhaps not tapping into what the child may know. As knowing the child's understanding level is essential before it is assumed that there are difficulties with word-finding, a useful test is the *British Picture Vocabulary Scale* (Dunn *et al.*, 1997). Used by SALTs, educational psychologists and teachers, it is a standardised individually administered picture test of receptive vocabulary for children aged 3 years to 15 years 8 months. Another assessment, the *Clinical Evaluation of Language Fundamentals* (*CELF*) *Test* (Semel *et al.*, 1997), yields scores for receptive and expressive language, language structure, language content and memory and working memory, and has subtests for skills such as phonological awareness, word associations and memory composites. While, in 2005, it had USA norms there were plans to develop UK norms.

The *Assessment of Comprehension and Expression 6–11* (Adams *et al.*, 2001), for use with children aged 6 years to 11 years 11 months, aims to identify children who have delays with or impairments to their comprehension or expression of language. Among other commercial assessments are the following.

◆ *Test of Word Finding* (German, 1986)

This is an assessment procedure for investigating a child's difficulties with meaning in language, and uses a confrontation naming approach. Developed in the USA, it contains American terms, limiting its use in English settings.

◆   *Understanding Ambiguity* (Rinaldi, 1996)

This assessment for children aged 8 to 11 years is untimed and intended to be used by speech and language therapists, educational psychologists, SENCOs and other staff working in language units. It includes an assessment (suitable for pupils aged 10 to 11 years) using homonyms, idiom, and phrases with multiple meanings, although it is not standardised.

Liaison between the teacher, SENCO and SALT

As already indicated, an experienced teacher's judgement about whether a pupil is progressing in developing an understanding of meaning in language will be useful. If concerns do arise, the teacher will usually raise the matter first with the SENCO, who may then or later contact a SALT or an educational psychologist for advice.

The teacher observation that has led to concerns being raised about a child's development in relation to meaning in language will continue as necessary, even after advice and support has been sought from the SENCO, the SALT or the educational psychologist. The teacher will need to continue observations to ensure that the pupil's development is satisfactory or to monitor the impact of any interventions.

Vocabulary assessment

Collecting and analysing a child's spontaneous vocabulary provides useful information, as long as it is sampled from a variety of settings, for example the home, several different subject lessons in school and different situations (group talk, whole-class sessions). The *British Picture Vocabulary Scale* (Dunn *et al.*, 1997), a standardised individually administered picture test of receptive vocabulary for children aged 3 years to 15 years 8 months, may also be used.

Word elicitation tasks for idiom

Where there are problems with the child's use and understanding of idiom, word elicitation tasks are used to show the words that a child retrieves in response to word stimuli. Children tend to choose words that co-occur with the stimulus word co-grammatically; for example, anticipating as chunks, 'play/toys'. Older learners retrieve words from the same word class as the stimulus words, anticipating, for example, 'play/work' as chunks.

Interventions

Improving labelling

Generally, from quite an early age, children begin to learn that everything has a lexical referent and children aged between 3 and 5 years are often notoriously very keen to know the names of things. Children who have difficulties with labelling may require individual tutoring to help them develop the skills and understanding necessary. This may include making links between the spoken word and the object, action or other phenomena in question. It may involve developing more securely their concepts through experience (having structured experience of many chairs of different sizes and shapes). The child who may not have developed the skills and understanding underpinning the labelling may need support and explicit teaching to direct attention to an object or event being labelled. He may require explicit teaching and extensive structured experiences to come to recognise object permanence.

The child with difficulties in labelling may need teaching that there are implied links between objects and events and pictures or other items (symbolisation). Among ways in which this can be developed is through pretend play (copying events such as washing, shopping and so on) and using pictures that represent objects or actions.

Should a child have difficulty storing the auditory information needed to make the links for labelling, he may benefit from the use of gesture or sign language. One example is 'Signalong' (for an outline of this and other sign systems, see Farrell, 2003, pp. 149–51). A potential advantage of sign systems is that auditory information can be linked with the tactile, kinaesthetic and visual features and memory, although sign systems are still symbolic and require a level of development commensurate with understanding this. Graphic symbols such as 'rebuses' may be used to aid labelling, in that they provide visual clues and draw on visual memory for a child who may have difficulties with auditory memory.

For a child having a sense of symbolising through play and the use of pictures but still having difficulty with learning words because of problems making sense of and storing auditory information, the use of picture matching, printed labels and sign language may lead to progress (Martin and Reilly, 1995).

If a child has word-finding difficulties (and assuming that understanding has been checked), he can be helped to identify his best word-finding strategies and encouraged to use them. If the child does not have word-finding strategies, he can be taught some; for example, using related words until the correct one is found ('I am looking for my . . . you wear them . . . you put them on your feet . . . mine are blue . . . *shoes*'). In being taught such a strategy, the teacher or SALT will indicate to the child that the word he may have chosen appears not to be the correct one and will then encourage the child to use the preferred strategy to retrieve the required word (Landells, 1989).

Helping packaging

Difficulties with under-extended conceptual meaning (e.g. 'dog' refers to only the child's dog) and overextended conceptual meaning (e.g. 'dog' refers to all small animals) may be helped by the adult carefully analysing and coming to understand the way in which the child perceives the concepts with which difficulties are identified. Only once this is done can misconceptions be corrected.

This process can be initiated in one-to-one sessions with the adult and the pupil. Extending under-extended concepts can begin with showing the pupil other examples of the under-extended concept. The child who uses 'dog' to refer only to his pet can be encouraged to talk about a photograph of his dog and then look at photographs of other dogs. Similar features can be pointed out that can extend the use of the word to other dogs. At first, these may be other dogs that are similar in appearance to the child's own pet (e.g. small, short-haired, long-tailed). This can be gradually extended to less similar dogs. Effectively, the child is being encouraged to generalise the concept of 'dog'.

Conversely, a pupil who has overextended conceptual meaning ('dog' might refer to all small animals) can be taught to make necessary discriminations to distinguish small animals that are not dogs. The child is taught to particularise. Again, using several photographs of dogs and several photographs of, say, rabbits may help this. The pupil is asked to look for ways in which the two are different (tail, ears, what they are eating). Other sets of photographs can be introduced gradually, once discriminations start to be made. The use of photographs can be extended so that, where possible, real animals are experienced.

Difficulties with the grammatical meaning aspect of packaging (understanding that the grammatical role of the word in a sentence affects its meaning) may be helped by directly teaching from exemplars, providing good models of the use of words in different grammatical roles and judiciously reshaping the child's utterances as appropriate, perhaps in time-limited sessions.

Helping networking

Difficulties with networking (the lexeme gaining meaning from its relationship with other words) relating to synonyms or antonyms can be taught explicitly, often as they arise in curriculum subjects. Similarly, explicit teaching of and checking understanding of subordinate and superordinate words and serial connections can all be explicitly taught and checked. Homonyms and homographs are likely to be taught in literacy work. Approaches that encourage semantic links such as Mind Maps™ may be used.

Difficulties with polysemy, where words are written and pronounced in the same way but have several meanings (e.g. 'top'), can be helped in various ways. The words can be taught and explained in their different subject contexts, perhaps using a few key words for each lesson, as appropriate. The meaning would be explained with reference to synonyms; for example, in science, 'class' would be explained in relation to 'group of substances', while in general school usage it would be taught as a 'group of pupils'. In this way the correct meaning is related to contextual clues in different school subjects. Particular difficulties can arise with recognising the abstract meaning of a polysemic word, in part because physical exemplars are not possible and because of the subtlety of the analogous use of the word. Such meanings can be discussed and directly taught, beginning with a concrete example of the word, such as 'sharp' as in blade, and moving on to 'sharp' as in taste (because the taste seems very concentrated, just as the blade is pressed into a small area).

Where a child has difficulty in learning the meaning of words, he may only know or remember one meaning of a word and may be confused if the word is used with another meaning. A useful strategy for this kind of difficulty is to teach the child a synonym or an antonym for the new meaning of the word. For example, a child may know the meaning of 'bill' as a request for payment but be confused when the word appears in reference to a bird. The new meaning can be taught by linking it to a synonym such as 'beak'. Or the word 'beak' may be chosen in preference to 'bill'. Difficulties with understanding that grammatical context can change the meaning of polysemic words can be helped by direct explicit teaching, using examples and discussing them with the pupil.

Helping the understanding of idiom

Understanding idiom can be helped by examples and explanations, and through analysing a child's processing. With regard to difficulties with idiom in which a word may be used in a figurative sense, these meanings will need to be explicitly taught, explained and discussed with a child who has difficulty with meanings. For example, the phrases 'he was cold towards her' or 'she gave him the cold shoulder' will be discussed and related to the more literal meaning of cold in temperature. Word elicitation tasks can be used to determine how children and young people with difficulties with idiom (and other multi-word strings) are storing and retrieving their meaning, in terms of analytic and holistic processing. Where this is done, the information can indicate suitable interventions.

Helping the understanding of grammar and meaning through direct teaching

Children who are having difficulty with meaning in language may also have difficulty in recognising that a word can have different meanings by being used in a different grammatical role. The point to be recognised is that, while a child begins to learn language by associating particular words with particular phenomena ('green' for the colour), this sort of association can be disturbed by the grammatical role of the word ('green' for the common areas of land in a village). The teacher can explain this feature of language and give examples followed by practice and assessment. Pupils will require specific teaching and support to develop an understanding of this feature of grammar.

Helping the understanding of meaning relations

Help in understanding meaning relations is gained through practice and exemplars, and through structured experiences and over-learning. Children having difficulties understanding that the meaning structure of a sentence can remain the same even though its grammatical structure may change will need support in two aspects. The first is in changing the grammatical structure while maintaining the meaning. Practice and exemplars may help this. The second is in maintaining the meaning when hearing utterances in which the grammatical structure is different to what was originally said or expected. Providing structured experience of these kinds of changes and allowing over-learning of the principles can assist.

THINKING POINTS

Readers may wish to consider:

◆ the extent to which teaching in a school routinely helps pupils to develop a grasp of word meaning;
◆ the effectiveness of strategies used where pupils have particular difficulties grasping word meaning.

KEY TEXT

Aitchison, J. (1987) *Words in the Mind: An Introduction to the Mental Lexicon*, Oxford, Basil Blackwell.

This book is aimed at teachers and SALTs as well as the general reader. Chapter 8 concerns how children acquire word meaning and discusses the 'labelling task', the 'packaging task' and 'network-building'.

Chapter 5

Difficulties with the use of language

INTRODUCTION

This chapter examines the use of language, pragmatics. I present various definitions of pragmatics. The chapter then considers five areas:

◆ certain basic knowledge and skills associated with pragmatics;
◆ grammatical sense in language use;
◆ social and linguistic sense;
◆ conversational skills in terms of such features as introducing a topic of conversation, maintaining it and concluding it;
◆ semantic–pragmatic issues.

I consider difficulties relating to pragmatics in these five areas and then examine identification and assessment in relation to pragmatics. I look at various interventions in relation to the five areas of difficulty and, finally, touch on issues pertinent to bilingual children.

What is pragmatics?

The nature of pragmatics is not easy to pin down. It has been considered to concern 'the skills we use to interact effectively, share meaning and communicate with each other' (Martin, 2000, p. 10). It has been stated that pragmatics 'covers all the ways in which the grammar serves the needs of speakers as social human beings' (Foster, 1990, pp. 6–7). It is 'The study of how expressions of meaning by humans gain significance in context and use' (Smith and Leinonen, 1992, p. 29). Pragmatics has been described as 'the study of the social use of language' (Anderson-Wood and Smith, 1997, p. 7) and the 'real life use and comprehension of flexible meanings' (p. 3). It will be seen from these definitions that pragmatics refers essentially to the use of language.

Making intelligible speech sounds, using grammar appropriately and using meaningful vocabulary are all of them important, as earlier chapters of this book have indicated. But, in order to communicate effectively, something more is required. When one is listening to another person, one has to interpret what is meant in a way that goes beyond the structural properties of language. This involves subtle skills and levels of understanding that are sometimes signalled by the expression 'reading between the lines'.

If these complex and subtle skills are important for a listener, they are equally vital for a speaker. We speak in a way that often suggests that we expect the listener to 'read between the lines' too. Language is used for different purposes, each purpose often requiring more than the literal content of the language used, as when making jokes, being sarcastic, witty or ironic, being polite and showing intimacy.

Pragmatic skills are necessary in different contexts. Anderson-Wood and Smith (1997, pp. 40–1), in looking at the complexities of assessing pragmatics, indicate such contexts, which are also helpful to consider in relation to developing a further understanding of pragmatics. The contexts they suggest are culture and subculture, situation, activity, role, relationship, the current state of the relationship, knowledge of partner, topic, linguistic context and inferential context.

According to their *culture and subculture*, people may have, for example, different ideas about what constitutes politeness and rudeness. If a pupil, at an age when others might expect some understanding of such differences, is insufficiently aware of them, he is more likely to be perceived by a communicative partner as impolite. It may be easier for some children to communicate more easily in some *situations* (home or school or youth group) than others. This may be in part because the child feels more at ease in some situations than in others and also because the topics and levels of shared understanding may be more accessible in one situation than another.

It tends to be easier to talk about current *activities* than those carried out some time ago. This is partly because, in current activities, objects and circumstances are visible at the time of speaking, providing a supportive context for communication. On the other hand, talking about what one did last week does not usually have such an enabling structure. Communication is likely to be different according to the *role* of the speaker, for example whether the speaker is communicating with an equal or someone in a position of authority. A child with pragmatic difficulties will not always grasp this and this will affect the response of the person they are addressing, which will in turn affect the child. One tends to communicate differently with people according to the *relationship*, for example how well one knows them, because the past history of the relationship provides reference points for communication that are not possible with others one knows less well. Also, communication is influenced by *the current state of the relationship*; for example, whether or not one is on friendly terms with the person with whom one is communicating.

The *knowledge of the partner* with whom one is communicating, such as what we take to be their emotional state and their knowledge, influences our communication with them. The *topic* of a person's communication is influential, for example whether one knows little or much about the topic or how complicated the topic is for most people. The *linguistic context* refers to what has gone before in the communication and how we respond to it. This implies that, for communication to be smooth, what is said must fit into the pattern of what has gone before; also, there has to be some sense of where the communication is going. As well as there being a grammatical structure to sentences, there is also a predictable structure to longer stretches of communication.

The *inferential context* refers to what one infers from what is said beyond the literal meanings of the words. This again is very difficult to convey in a set of rigid rules. It involves indicating that one has understood the communicative partner's apparent intention, as well as the literal words he or she has spoken. This implies considering the significance as well as the literal meaning of what has been said by both people.

Using language effectively, then, depends on understanding meaning but also on understanding the appropriateness of language as communication in different contexts.

Aspects of pragmatics

Basic skills and knowledge

Among basic skills and knowledge associated with pragmatics are the developing ability and motivation to interact, for example, with another person initiating an interaction, or to take part in some group activity, such as saying a rhyme or singing a song. Sharing attention is important.

Grammatical sense in language use

Grammatical cohesion is achieved as utterances are linked with one another to avoid unnecessary repetition, draw on shared assumptions and understanding and keep the listener's interest. Among the ways in which such cohesion is achieved are reference, substitutions and conjunctions. 'Reference' uses grammatical short forms, for example, to carry information over from earlier utterances, as when recurring words or phrases are replaced by a pronoun. 'Substitution' involves substituting for an already used word another word or phrase conveying the same meaning, as in the utterance 'I lost my *calculator and compass* and now I can't do the maths test because I don't have the *equipment*.' 'Conjunctions' join utterances to avoid repetition, so, to avoid saying 'Robert went to the shops. Robert went to the post office. Robert went to the cinema', one would say 'Robert went to the shops, the post office and the cinema.'

Social and linguistic sense

For utterances to make social and linguistic sense, important features are the intentions of the speaker, a shared understanding between speaker and listener, and inference and implication.

Speaker's intention relates to speaking for a purpose, such as to ask a question or to make a criticism. Shared understanding of the context of an utterance concerns the speaker and listener understanding to whom they are communicating. Inference and implication involve the speakers and listeners understanding and being able to respond suitably to various conventions, such as polite but indirect requests. For example, to understand someone at the table saying 'Is there any salt down there?', it is usually necessary to realise that what they are implying is 'Please pass me the salt.'

Conversational skills

Conversational skills involve being able to use suitable grammatical forms to convey information, as already explained, using such devices as reference, substitutions and conjunctions. Also, conversation involves the ability to:

◆ introduce a topic of conversation, maintain it and conclude it;
◆ take turns in conversation as speaker or listener and take turns initiating new topics;
◆ adopt a suitable manner of address (such as formal or informal) using the appropriate tone;
◆ repair a conversation if it breaks down, for example because of misunderstanding, by perhaps seeking to clarify the confusion;
◆ convey information, including that about other times and places and hypothetical situations;
◆ use non-verbal communication such as eye contact, facial expression and bodily proximity appropriately.

Semantic–pragmatic issues

It will be remembered from Chapter 4: 'Difficulties with meaning', that semantics concerns the meaning of language and that a word or several words (lexeme) can be used when intending the same meaning. For the lexeme to be meaningful, the speaker has to have a certain amount of knowledge of concepts. Furthermore, to grasp the meaning of lexemes implies that other cognitive factors support the understanding of meaning. The context in which the word is used is also an indication that the child has grasped its meaning and the context is therefore a part of our understanding of meaning. Semantic–pragmatic issues therefore concern the interaction of pragmatic skills and knowledge, and skills and knowledge relating to semantics.

Difficulties with pragmatics

It has been suggested that 'Pragmatic dysfunction differs from other disturbances of communication in that it primarily concerns communication *in context*' (Anderson-Wood and Smith, 1997, p. 31, italics in original). Also, 'because the difficulty arises within an interaction, both partners in the interaction can contribute towards its failure or success' (p. 31). Pragmatic difficulties may affect both expressive and receptive pragmatic abilities. Difficulties in using language have to do with difficulties with understanding language meaning but, equally, concern difficulties with the 'cognitive and emotional understanding of communicative appropriateness in social contexts' (Martin and Miller, 2003, p. 104).

Difficulties with basic skills and knowledge

A child may have difficulties with basic skills and knowledge associated with pragmatics, such as sharing attention, or the ability and desire to interact with another person or to take part in some group activity.

Difficulties with grammatical sense in language use

As indicated earlier, grammatical cohesion is achieved as utterances are linked with one another to avoid unnecessary repetition, to draw on shared assumptions and understanding and to keep the listener's interest through such devices as reference, substitutions and conjunctions. Difficulties will be evident where a child is unable to use such devices.

Difficulties with social and linguistic sense

For a child having difficulty with the social and linguistic sense of utterances, there may be difficulties understanding the intentions of the speaker, a lack of shared understanding between speaker and listener, and difficulties with inference and implication. These are likely to lead to the pupil responding inappropriately to utterances and finding it difficult to keep meaningful exchanges going.

Difficulties with conversational skills

Difficulties relating to topic in conversation may be indicated when a pupil tends to change the topic more than is usual or appears restless. Or the pupil may, in response to a topic being initiated by another person, respond tersely and be disinclined to extend the topic or introduce a new one. The pupil may not understand the signals conveying that a topic is being introduced.

A child having difficulties with turn-taking conversation may interrupt or fail to pick up signals that the other person wants a turn. Where a child has not learned how to adapt forms of address to different situations and different people, he may, for example, speak condescendingly to adults or be over-formal to other children. A child may have difficulty in recognising that a conversation is breaking down because of misunderstandings or interruptions and so on, and have difficulty in repairing the conversation, for example by asking clarifying questions or seeking to pick up where the conversation left off. Where a child contributes to the breakdown of the conversation, he may have difficulty realising this. Difficulties may be experienced with conversational abstractions. While conversation can, of course, be about the here and now, the greater challenge and the greater likelihood of difficulties arise when the conversation concerns matters that are not in the here and now, or that involve reference to emotional states, hypothetical situations or causal links. Particular difficulties may be experienced in subjects such as history, which by definition is not about the now, even if it is about the 'here', and geography, which may be about the 'now' but not the 'here'. Difficulties with non-verbal communication may relate to problems with using appropriate facial expression, bodily proximity (standing neither too close nor too far away from a conversational partner), using gestures appropriately, and matching body language and verbal language.

Semantic–pragmatic difficulties

Some children have problems with both meaning in language and language use and these are referred to as 'semantic–pragmatic difficulties'. Semantic–pragmatic disorder is considered to be a developmental language disorder concerning language meaning and function. Children with pragmatic difficulties 'only' do not necessarily have behaviours associated with ASD. They have primary difficulties with communication and conversation but may not have difficulties with other aspects of language such as grammar. They tend to have (like children with semantic–pragmatic difficulties) problems staying on a conversational topic, turn-taking difficulties, and cannot always sufficiently take account of the knowledge of their conversational partner.

Causal factors

It has been suggested that among possible causes of pragmatic difficulties are the following:

1   semantic difficulties;
2   impairment of cognition;
3   impairment of imagination;
4   institutionalisation;
5   negative environmental influences . . . ;
6   lack of social experience possibly playing a part in the development of appropriate styles of interaction;
7   certain neurological conditions, particularly those affecting the right hemi-sphere.

(Anderson-Wood and Smith, 1997, p. 32)

Identification and assessment

Different levels of severity have been suggested with regard to pragmatic difficulties. For example, severe pragmatic difficulties may be experienced by people with autism or some kind of psychosis. Moderate pragmatic difficulty might include, for example, children with speech/language delays or disorders who lack basic communicative competence. Mild pragmatic difficulty might include people who lack conversational 'know how', which could apply to most people at some time (Anderson-Wood and Smith, 1997, p. 35).

National Curriculum

At Key Stage 1, the National Curriculum guidance states that pupils should be taught, in speaking, to 'take into account the needs of their listeners' and, in listening, to 'make relevant comments', 'sustain concentration', 'listen to others' reactions' and 'ask questions to clarify their understanding'. In group discussions and interaction, pupils should be taught to 'take turns in speaking' and 'relate their contribution to what has gone before' (DfEE/QCA, 1999a, p. 44). At Key Stage 2, pupils should be taught, in speaking, to 'choose material that is relevant to the topic and to the listeners'. In listening, they should be taught to 'ask relevant questions to clarify, extend and follow up ideas' and 'respond to others appropriately, taking into account what they say' (p. 50). For Key Stages 3 and 4, in speaking, the pupil should be taught to 'use gesture, tone, pace and rhetorical devices for emphasis' and 'evaluate the effectiveness of their speech and consider how to adapt it to a range of situations'. In listening, the pupil should be taught to 'distinguish tone, undertone, implications and other signs of speakers' intentions' and 'ask questions and give relevant and helpful comments'. In group discussion and interaction, pupils should be taught to 'make different types of contribution to groups, adapting their speech to their listeners and the activity' (DfEE/QCA, 1999b, p. 46).

These guidelines for teaching, taken with the relevant attainment targets for speaking and listening, give a very broad indication of what might be expected of children at different ages. The teacher's experience will also be brought to bear as she considers whether, for a particular child, there are any reasons for concern.

Informal assessments

The identification of pragmatic dysfunction has been said to begin with 'subjective feelings of discomfort on the part of communicative partners' (Anderson-Wood and Smith, 1997, p. 32). Among the informal assessments relevant to pupils with pragmatic difficulties is the assessment of conversational skills. As the earlier sections have indicated, difficulties can be evident with conversational skills relating to topic, turn-taking, conversational address, repair and abstractions. To gain a baseline assessment of the child's skills, observations and recording of such conversational skills can be made in different contexts, perhaps using audio-tape recordings or video recordings (which allow the social setting to be seen and non-verbal communication to be assessed). The importance of gathering information in different contexts relates to the variability of children's communication in different settings such as the home, the school and the clinic (Stacey, 1994). Progress can be monitored by repeating the process of gathering this information at agreed intervals.

Tests, checklists and profiles

Among tests used in relation to pupils' difficulties with pragmatics is the *Children's Communication Checklist* (Bishop, 1998). This seeks to distinguish between, on the one hand, children whose main difficulty is in understanding language, which leads to difficulties in communicating, and, on the other hand, children having pragmatic difficulties. It therefore rates communication and social behaviour and identifies social difficulties as well as identifying problems with language. Another assessment is *The Pragmatic Profile of Everyday Communication Skills in School Aged Children* (Dewart and Summers, 1995). This includes gathering information relating to different aspects of the child's communication at home. Nursery and school staff also can be interviewed to provide information about the child's communication in these contexts. Two assessments intended for older primary school pupils and secondary-aged pupils having pragmatic difficulties are:

◆ the *Social Use of Language Programme* (*SULP*) (Rinaldi, 1992), which has a communication skills rating chart;
◆ the *CELF Test* (Semel *et al.*, 1997).

Identifying and distinguishing pragmatic difficulties and semantic–pragmatic difficulties

Attempts have been made to identify and distinguish pragmatic difficulties and semantic–pragmatic difficulties. Regarding children considered to have semantic–pragmatic difficulties, there are considered to be some similarities with children identified as having ASD. Indeed, it is debated whether semantic–pragmatic disorders should be considered separately from ASD (Gagnon *et al.*, 1997). Such children may be over-literal in their attempts to make inferences, have a primary difficulty with semantic knowledge and may also have difficulties with grammar. They have difficulties with word-finding, learning vocabulary and auditory comprehension. Poor socialising skills restrict socialising with peers, which may lead to less and less participation with them.

Interventions

Providing basic skills and knowledge

Among basic interventions that may be suitable for children with severe pragmatic difficulties are interactive games, communication facilitation techniques (CFTs) and naturalistic interventions. Interactive games include such activities as peek-a-boo and rhymes or songs with repeated sounds and movements. CFTs seek to be very responsive to the child's communicative attempts. 'The CFTs aim to encourage the adult to shift attention away from the speech performance of the client and direct it towards the client's interests and choice of activities' (Anderson-Wood and Smith, 1997, p. 80). These can be used at a pre-linguistic level (e.g. sharing attention), the linguistic stage (e.g. repeating what the pupil says), and the complex language stage (e.g. making a statement that is likely to lead to the child saying something). Naturalistic interventions 'provide opportunities for genuine interaction' (p. 85). One aspect of this is 'contingent responding', which involves sensitively and alertly responding to what the child says or indicates.

Helping with difficulties with grammatical sense in language use

Where a child has difficulty with grammatical cohesion devices such as reference, substitutions and conjunctions, intervention can involve the SALT (or the teacher or teaching assistant working with the SALT) providing models of these and helping the child to practise them, perhaps in role-play settings.

Helping with difficulties with social and linguistic sense

A child may have difficulties understanding the intentions of the speaker, may lack a shared understanding between speaker and listener, and may have difficulties with inference and implication. Interventions can include being taught possible signals of the speaker's intentions and examples of inference and implication. Opportunities to use similar signals can be provided in role-play and encouraged when they appear in day-to-day communication. The *SULP* (Rinaldi, 2001) is used for assessment, as has been indicated earlier. It also provides a teaching framework to develop language skills in real-life settings and teaches the basic social communication skills and an awareness of self and others. The programme is suitable to be used by SALTs, SENCOs, educational psychologists, teachers and teaching assistants.

Helping with difficulties with conversational skills

If a pupil has difficulty with the topic aspect of conversation, this may be because he does not understand the signals that a topic is being introduced. A common indication that a new topic is intended is the use of open-ended questions ('What did you think of the film last night?'). The child can be taught to recognise this gambit and to respond accordingly, for example by asking a question ('You mean the horror film?') or commenting from his own experience ('I thought it was good but not as good as *Dracula*'). The child may tend not to recognise when someone is trying to round off a conversation and may have difficulty signalling politely that he wants to end a topic of conversation himself. Again, the child can be taught to listen for possible signals that someone would like to change the subject ('I liked the school trip too, but I don't think I told you about the visit from my aunt.'). He can learn and practise more subtle ways of indicating a desire to change topic himself.

A child having difficulties with turn-taking in conversation can be taught the signals that the other person wants a turn (e.g. a pause or a question) and to respond to them and also to use the signals themselves. Role-play and encouragement when such devices appear in day-to-day communication can be a help.

Where a child has not learned the conversational forms of address for different situations and different people, the teacher or other adult can pick this up as it arises and point it out to the child. It is important that this is done in a way that encourages the child and builds rather than diminishes confidence. As well as explaining how and why the form of address is not suitable, the adult should provide examples of how it can be made more apt. Of course, the child should be praised for attempts that approach what is expected.

Where a child finds it hard to recognise that a conversation is breaking down and has difficulty repairing it, the signs of conversation breakdown can be explained and the skills of repairing it (e.g. clarifying questions) can be taught. Where a child contributes to the breakdown of the conversation and has difficulty realising this, the adult can signal the breakdown, for example by saying that she does not understand and by asking a clarifying question or using some other repair strategy.

Helping a pupil who has difficulty with conversational abstractions has implications for all areas of the curriculum but may be more apparent in particular subjects. Where a child has difficulty with conversations that concern other places and times, emotional states, hypothetical situations or causal links, specific support may be needed for these subjects, such as pre-teaching some of the concepts.

Help with difficulties with non-verbal communication will take into account its culturally variable nature. Teaching non-verbal communication is not easy as it is subtle and timing is also important; but some progress can be made through the teacher or others seeking to model suitable non-verbal communication, helping the child to practise it through role-play, and encouraging and praising approximations to more suitable body language as the child shows it in day-to-day communication.

Help with semantic–pragmatic difficulties

With regard to children considered to have semantic–pragmatic difficulties, poor socialising skills restrict socialising with peers, which may lead to less and less participation with them. It is particularly important that these pupils have help with communication interaction skills in the early years and at school. Support in the family is also important. If assessment indicates that a main influence of the difficulties stem from semantic difficulties that lead to and compound pragmatic difficulties, interventions may include those intended to improve semantic skills, for example developing phonological awareness skills through such means as over-learning and practising phonological awareness tasks.

Bilingual children

A child who is brought up in a linguistic minority community may learn the home language first and English later, perhaps beginning at school. If so, the child will tend to develop the skills of communication associated with his first language. These skills may be interpreted as difficulties in the English-speaking context; for example, if it is acceptable that a child responds minimally in his first language community, this may be seen as a potential communication difficulty in the school context. The teacher's close liaison with the specialist teachers supporting the child's learning of English will help in determining whether a child has pragmatic difficulties or whether the language behaviour reflects the different expectations of various language communities. Where there appear to be pragmatic difficulties, it is important in all cases to gather a range of information from different contexts. This is because, for the bilingual child, these contexts will include not only different situations but also different linguistic communities.

THINKING POINTS

Readers may wish to consider in the case of a particular school:

◆ the extent to which the existing curriculum encourages and develops pupils' pragmatic skills;
◆ how pragmatic difficulties are identified and assessed;
◆ the degree to which further explicit intervention is necessary for pupils who find difficulty with pragmatics.

KEY TEXT

Anderson-Wood, L. and Smith, B. R. (1997) *Working with Pragmatics: A Practical Guide to Promoting Communicative Confidence*, Bicester, Winslow Press.

This book is addressed mainly to SALTs and encourages an approach to working therapeutically while involving day-to-day communication in real-life contexts. This aims to help the client generalise what is learned and used. The book suggests that SALTs work in situations that create a wish and a need to communicate. The emphasis on everyday communication and real contexts opens up opportunities for teachers working with SALTs to support pupils who have difficulty with pragmatics.

Chapter 6

Difficulties with comprehension

INTRODUCTION

To 'comprehend' something is to grasp and to understand it and the term also conveys some notion of breadth and of embracing a subject or a situation. This chapter explains a framework for analysing comprehension in which it is seen as a process whereby information is transformed from one kind of representation to another. I look at difficulties with comprehension, considering, in turn, attention, problems in discriminating sounds, understanding the grammar of utterances, and difficulties related to cognitive skills. The chapter considers the identification and assessment of comprehension difficulties in terms of Foundation Stage assessments, National Curriculum expectations, liaison between the teacher, the SENCO and the SALT, formal assessments, and medical identification.

I explain several interventions aiming to assist and develop language comprehension and their rationale. These include explicit teaching for (and reminders of) giving attention; teaching listening behaviour; helping with difficulties understanding grammar; checking specific areas of understanding; encouraging pupil assertiveness to signal lack of comprehension; and using different senses and other aids. The chapter also advocates clear teacher communication, allowing the pupil time to respond, support as necessary for the particular language demands of different school subjects, and ensuring that poor comprehension of language is not wrongly interpreted as misbehaviour.

As comprehension concerns the *understanding* of speech, grammar, meaning and pragmatics, much of what has been discussed in earlier chapters, including interventions, may be borne in mind.

Comprehension-transforming 'representations'

A framework for analysing comprehension can be outlined that envisages a process ranging from sound to meaning. In a simplified model, comprehension is seen as 'a process whereby information is successfully transformed from one kind of *representation* to another' (Bishop, 1997, p. 2, italics added).

When a sound is made, and when a person speaks, sound waves are produced that are channelled through the hearer's ear canal to the middle ear. Sound waves of different frequencies reach the tympanic membrane (eardrum) between the outer and middle ears, causing the membrane to vibrate at different speeds. Through mechanisms in the middle ear, vibrations are transmitted to the 'oval window' membrane and thence to the basilar membrane of the cochlea (in the inner ear). The vibrations of the basilar membrane stimulate microscopic hair cells, which feed impulses into the auditory nerve. The auditory nerve and subcortical systems convey what Bishop (1997) calls 'neurally encoded *representations*' of the frequency and intensity qualities of the sound to the auditory cortex of the brain (p. 4, italics added).

In the auditory cortex, some brain cells fire selectively in response to sounds of certain frequencies while other brain cells respond to changes in frequency over a given range or direction. This responsiveness to certain frequencies is some-times described as the 'neural spectrogram' (p. 9). There appears to be an intermediate level of *representation* between the 'neural spectrogram' (p. 9) and word recognition, although the outcome is that the brain interprets the stream of sounds into the discrete units of individual words.

Some children aged 5 or 6 years seem unable to match or identify phonemes and therefore find difficulty in learning letter–sound correspondences, but have no obvious difficulties in understanding or producing speech (p. 9). Such difficulties may relate to lack of one-to-one correspondence between segments of the acoustic signal and phonemes (Liberman *et al.*, 1989). Early phonological development may involve progression from larger units of analysis to more finely grained ones. At first, the child may 'operate with whole words or even short phrases, simply encoding these in terms of certain salient features, such as number of syllables, stress, and the presence of phonetic features' (p. 9) (see also Walley, 1993). By the age of 3 or 4 years, most children seem aware of the subsyllabic units of onset and rime. Later, perhaps after being exposed to print, they recognise the smaller phonemic elements.

The child developing language identifies, from the flow of speech, recurring and meaningful patterns and stores these in long-term memory so that, when they are heard again, they are recognised as known words. Mental *representations* of words have information about both the word's phonological form and a repre-sentation of its meaning. Acquiring vocabulary can be seen as involving storing representations of familiar sequences of speech sounds in a mental 'lexicon' and associating these with particular meanings. Items in the mental lexicon are matched with sequences of sounds in the incoming speech signal.

An incoming sentence must be parsed into phrases that correspond to units of meaning, and the relationships between these have to be decoded (Bishop, 1997, p. 11). Syntax and morphology describe this grammatical sequencing for meaning. Understanding sentences also requires the ability to use knowledge of grammar in 'real time' to interpret utterances. The interpretation of an utterance at all levels is made clearer by drawing on general knowledge of the world to infer what is meant in a given context (p. 12). The understanding of discourse (long stretches of talk) also informs interpretations. To understand an utterance, it is necessary often to go beyond the interpretation of the sequence of words and to bring to bear interpretations about the speaker's intentions. Otherwise, aspects of communication such as humour, sarcasm, metaphor and so on are beyond understanding. Children with autism find this pragmatic aspect of understanding very difficult.

Difficulties with comprehension and their causes

Where a pupil has difficulties with comprehension, these may relate to attention problems, problems discriminating sounds, difficulties understanding grammar, difficulties understanding the pragmatic aspect of communication and more general cognitive difficulties.

Where a child has difficulties with attention, he may have visual or hearing impairment and so for physical reasons finds it difficult to control attention. For some children it may be that the maturation of their nervous system is slower than usual, leading to slower development of learning the skills of listening, looking and maintaining attention. If a child is unable to control his attention, and is attracted to and distracted by non-relevant sights and sounds in his environment, he will find it difficult to direct attention to the teacher's instructions (e.g. Thompson, 2003, p. 57). The difficulties may manifest themselves more in one situation than another; for example, the child may find it more difficult to maintain attention in a whole-class setting than in a small group.

Children may experience problems with different aspects of language such as discriminating between different sounds. This can mean that the child does not receive sufficient information necessary to comprehend an utterance in the first place.

A child with difficulties in understanding adult-like grammar may have problems with necessary information storage and retrieval, particularly when the sequence of utterances does not reflect the sequence of events they convey. The hierarchical structure of some utterances tends to make processing more difficult. Sometimes, a child may have a more limited short-term auditory memory than most.

Where a child has difficulties in understanding pragmatic aspects of communication, the problems may extend to incorrectly interpreting other people's non-verbal communication, not understanding intention – for example when humour or sarcasm is used – and having difficulty with other non-literal expressions.

If a child has difficulties with comprehension, difficulties with cognitive skills may be implicated, for example involving auditory processing or sequencing and recalling what is heard. If auditory processing is slower that usual, the child may well be trying to understand one part of an utterance while the speaker is continuing with further information that is therefore likely to be missed or only partially grasped.

Identification and assessment

There is the potential for difficulties with attention and comprehension to be incorrectly interpreted by the teacher as bad behaviour. If a child does not understand a request, he will be unable to carry it out, which can be misconstrued as defiance or as being unco-operative. Should the child take longer than others to respond to a question from the teacher because he has difficulty processing the information, the teacher might assume that the child has not been listening and therefore does not know the answer. If, on top of the child's difficulties, the teacher or others misconstrue such behaviours as unco-operative or naughty, the pupil's difficulties are likely to be compounded and his frustrations increased. It is, therefore, important that comprehension difficulties are identified correctly and that suitable support is provided. The identification and assessment of difficulties with comprehension include judgements made in the Foundation Stage of schooling, National Curriculum expectations, liaison between the teacher, the SENCO and the SALT, assessing difficulties in attention, formal assessments and medical identification.

Foundation Stage assessments

Provision in the early years involves the teacher and others providing opportunities for the pupil to develop in six areas of learning, including 'communication, language and literacy' and 'knowledge and understanding of the world'. Early learning goals specify what most children are expected to have achieved in the six areas of learning by the end of the Foundation Stage. Difficulties with comprehension may therefore be identified within the Foundation Stage assessments, although this tends to be a difficult area to assess.

National Curriculum expectations

There is perhaps insufficient emphasis on understanding/comprehension in the National Curriculum, making it important that the teacher makes the best use of opportunities to develop and check pupils' comprehension. National Curriculum programmes of study for Key Stage 1 (5–7-year-olds) for listening include that the child should be taught to 'sustain concentration', 'listen to others' reactions' and 'ask questions to clarify their understanding'. In group discussions, the pupil should be taught to 'take turns in speaking' and 'relate their contributions to what has gone before' (DfEE/QCA, 1999a, p. 44).

At Key Stage 2 (age 7–11), pupils should be taught to 'ask relevant questions to clarify, extend and follow up ideas', 'recall and re-present important features of an argument, talk, reading, radio or television programme, film' and 'respond to others appropriately, taking into account what they say'. In discussions involving groups, pupils should be taught to 'make contributions relevant to the topic and take turns in discussion' (p. 50).

Key Stages 3 and 4 (ages 11–16) require that pupils be taught to:

- 'concentrate on and recall the main features of a talk, reading, radio or television programme',
- 'identify the major elements of what is being said both explicitly and implicitly',
- 'distinguish features of presentation where a speaker aims to explain, persuade, amuse or argue a case',
- 'distinguish tone, undertone and implications and other signs of a speaker's intentions',

◆ 'recognise when a speaker is being ambiguous or deliberately vague, glosses over points, uses and abuses evidence and makes unsubstantiated statements' and

◆ 'ask questions and give relevant and helpful comments'.

(DfEE/QCA, 1999b, p. 46)

To the extent that the programmes of study imply that most pupils will develop skills and understanding as a result of this teaching, as is reflected in the National Curriculum attainment targets, teachers will notice pupils who have particular difficulties with these aspects of comprehension and will take action as necessary.

Liaison between the teacher, the SENCO and the SALT

Systematic classroom observation will indicate a child's difficulties with comprehension and these can, if there is initial concern, be compared with information on the child's apparent comprehension of language in the home. Particular note will be made of how the child responds to the language of the teacher, other adults and other children in relation to, for example, the child's name being used, requests being made of them, and so on, in different settings and with different people. Videotaping the child's response and the setting can provide useful information. To avoid anxiety, this should be explained and carried out with the child's co-operation, so that the child is a central part of the assessment process.

For example, in order to gain a fuller picture of a child's difficulties with attention, it will be necessary to observe the child in different settings. These can include activity in a class, in small groups and in different lessons of different content. The observations can include sessions having different potential sources of interest, such as visual or auditory stimuli and so on. Not only will such observations indicate areas of difficulty; they will also suggest areas of relative strength that can be used for subsequent intervention.

Where the teacher has concerns that a child is not able to understand language at a level commensurate with his age and is not progressing well, these may be raised with the SENCO. As necessary, the SENCO may make her own observations and may call upon the SALT to consider further assessment and advice.

Formal assessments

Among tests used to assess understanding of language is *The British Picture Vocabulary Scale* (Dunn *et al.*, 1997). Used by SALTs, educational psychologists and teachers, it is a standardised individually administered picture test of receptive vocabulary for children aged 3 years to 15 years 8 months. The *CELF Test* (Semel *et al.*, 1997) provides assessments of receptive and expressive language, language structure, language content and memory, and working memory and has subtests for skills such as phonological awareness, word associations and memory composites. The *Derbyshire Rapid Screening Test* (Knowles and Masidlover, 1987) is used for looking at a child's ability to use the word order of utterances to assist understanding. Other formal assessments of comprehension in language include the following:

◆ The comprehension scale of the *Reynell Developmental Language Scales* (Edwards *et al.*, 1997)

This relates to key information words and word order strategy, but the scale does not primarily assess grammatical structure.

◆ *Listening Comprehension Test Series* (Hagues *et al.*, 1999)

This is intended for children aged 4 to 14 and may be used by the SENCO and teacher as well as by an educational psychologist. It is a series of spoken standardised tests intended to help the teacher assess a pupil's progress in listening comprehension.

◆ *The Assessment of Comprehension and Expression 6–11* (Adams *et al.*, 2001)

This assesses language development in the areas of sentence comprehension, inferential comprehension, naming, syntactic formulation, semantic decisions, non-literal comprehension and narrative. Intended for use by SALTs and educational psychologists, the assessment takes approximately 30–45 mins to complete, but is often completed in two shorter sessions.

For bilingual pupils, assessments may be developed in the pupil's first linguistic community language as well as in English, as happens in Wales, where bilingual curriculum assessments are routinely made. Assessments in both of the child's languages allow the strengths and weaknesses of the child's understanding (and expression) to be investigated. They are likely to indicate whether the difficulties relate to one language or both.

Medical identification

Medical perspectives and medical diagnosis can inform the understanding of difficulties that include problems with comprehension. In so-called 'verbal auditory agnosia' or 'severe receptive/expressive syndrome', the child cannot make sense of speech sounds or other sounds. It may also appear as though the pupil has a hearing impairment, even though the child's hearing is normal. Genetic factors or acquired epilepsy syndrome may bring about this condition and verbal auditory agnosia is also associated with autism.

Interventions

The following interventions focus on prerequisites such as attention, as well as on other aspects of comprehension. They are: explicit teaching for (and reminders of) giving attention; modelling and other ways of teaching listening behaviour; helping with difficulties in understanding grammar; checking specific areas of understanding; support with pragmatic aspects of understanding; encouraging pupil assertiveness to signal lack of comprehension; and using different senses and other aids. I also look at clear teacher communication; allowing the pupil time to respond; support as necessary for the particular language demands of different school subjects; and ensuring that poor comprehension of language is not wrongly interpreted as misbehaviour.

Explicit teaching for (and reminders of) giving attention

Observation and assessment of the pupil may have indicated the different situations and stimuli that tend to capture or fail to capture the child's attention. This information is used to inform interventions. For example, if the child pays attention better to visual than to auditory stimuli, visual clues can be linked to auditory ones to help attract and maintain attention. The teacher can help ensure the attention of a particular pupil by naming him when giving instructions and by questioning the pupil to check that he was paying attention. Such an approach is good practice for all pupils, so there should be no suggestion that a pupil with difficulties is being singled out. Among suggestions to develop attention skills (Thompson, 2003, pp. 58–9) are for the teacher to keep language simple, providing visual cues of sequences and instructions such as a series of pictures, and rewarding good listening – perhaps through praise or the award of a sticker.

Teaching listening behaviour

Related to teaching and support in giving attention is the explicit teaching of listening behaviour. The child can be taught the usual prerequisites of listening, such as sitting still, not fidgeting, looking at the speaker and watching the speaker's gestures as well as listening to what is said verbally. A teacher or a LSA can model listening behaviour. Humour can be injected into the role-play by having the teacher or LSA model poor listening skills and ask the pupils to comment on how good the listening was and how it could be improved. The pupils, either with an adult or with another pupil, then practise the good listening skills, which are monitored and praised by the teacher. As the pupil spontaneously demonstrates good listening skills in other settings, these should be recognised and praised by the teacher and others. Listening skills can be introduced and practised through the following activities (taken from Thompson, 2003):

Identifying sounds

Identifying sounds can be practised, for example by using a cassette audio-tape of various farm, urban or domestic sounds where the pupil matches the sound to a picture. Speech sounds can be used similarly, where the pupil listens to various speakers and tries to guess their gender, age or other features. Anticipating and discriminating sounds in music lessons can make a valuable contribution to general listening skills.

Listening for a correct single speech sound

Once the child has practised a sound (for example, 's') and the teacher is sure that it is known, the child is given two or three pictures (e.g. indicating 'tea', 'sea', 'pea'). The teacher asks the child to be ready to point to the one *starting* with a specified sound (for example, 's') when the teacher says the word. The teacher then places a small screen between her and the pupil, so that the pupil cannot see the teacher's mouth, and says the three words. The pupil would of course be expected to indicate the picture of 'sea'. Using a similar structure, practice can also be given in listening for the final consonants of words.

The auditory discrimination of two similar sounds

In developing auditory discrimination of similar sounds, the sounds involved might be p/b, s/sk, t/d and k/g. The child is given pairs of picture cards (e.g. 'pear' and 'bear') and listens to the teacher saying one of the words before indicating the correct picture corresponding to that word.

Initial sounds

To encourage the child to listen to initial sounds, the teacher can give the child two letter cards with a related picture to give a visual prompt. One card might show the letter/sound 'f' with a picture of a fish. The other card might show the letter/sound 'th' with a picture of a thumb. The teacher says the word and the pupil says the letter/sound with which the word begins.

(Thompson, 2003, pp. 30–3, 59–61, paraphrased)

Helping with difficulties in understanding grammar

A child struggling with understanding adult-like grammar, who appears to be having difficulties with the storage and retrieval of the necessary information, may be helped if the teacher uses single phrase utterances. Where longer utterances are used, it helps if the teacher tries to ensure that the sequence supports understanding. For example, requests can be made to correspond to the order in which they are to be followed. 'Please put away the equipment and then go outside quietly' would be easier to understand and comply with than, 'before you go outside quietly, please put away the equipment'. A pupil having difficulties with understanding the grammatical aspects of an utterance is likely to find it easier to grasp key words that convey concrete meaning. The pupil may therefore pick up the word 'equipment' most easily and perhaps 'go outside'. If the context makes the meaning clear, the request is part of a usual routine and the child sees others complying with the request, the pupil is especially likely to understand. Because contextual clues as to the meaning of an utterance can help comprehension, 'here and now' utterances tend to be easier to understand than ones that concern the past, the future or other places.

Support with pragmatic areas of understanding

Helping the pupil to recognise some of the messages that might otherwise be missed can provide some support for difficulties with pragmatic understanding. Role-play sessions or video/DVD examples can illustrate the more usual examplars of the more obvious aspects of non-verbal communication, which can be discussed with a group of pupils. Examples of intention can be provided and discussed, so that an understanding of aspects of communication, such as humour and sarcasm, can begin to develop. The more common non-literal expressions can be explained, discussed and practised in role-play. The pervasiveness, variety and subtlety of pragmatic aspects of language are so complex that improving understanding in this is likely to be a long-term process.

Checking specific areas of understanding

Understanding can be checked through questions directed at specific pupils, particularly questions that establish understanding of the main points of the lesson, key words, the main learning points, the sequence of events in a story and so on. This is made more effective when the good practice is adopted of making clear to the pupils at the beginning of the lesson what the learning objectives are, of writing key words for all to see and explaining them. Not only should it be made clear to the pupils what the teacher expects them to have learned by the end of the lesson, but it should also be made clear what this means for particular pupils. Where this is deeply embedded as a teaching and learning strategy, even young pupils will tend to draw the teacher's attention to occasions in the lesson when they are not learning what the teacher said they would.

Encouraging pupil assertiveness to signal lack of comprehension

The teacher can encourage a pupil for whom comprehension may be a difficulty to signal when the teacher or others are not communicating clearly enough for the pupil to understand. Putting the responsibility for clear communication on the teacher and asking for the help of the pupil when the teacher's communication is opaque can help this. The signal from the pupil can be public or discreet (e.g. a privately agreed signal such as a card of a certain colour being lifted up). It helps if the pupil is seated where the teacher can easily see her.

Encouraging the pupil to use and talk about different senses and providing other aids

Comprehension can be helped by the teacher using visual aids and encouraging pupils to use other channels of communication such as touch, taste and smell to reinforce the usual mode of auditory comprehension. For some pupils, signing may be used to encourage kinaesthetic and visual memory to supplement comprehension. Helping the pupil to develop a vocabulary for taste, smell and touch can help comprehension in the sense of further developing information about the pupil's experiences and the environment and relating it to language. Communication boards and information and communication technology can assist comprehension. Reading and writing can also help, providing, as they do, visual information to supplement the auditory.

Clear teacher communication

The teacher should ensure that she is using her own language in a way that is likely to aid comprehension rather than obfuscate it; for example, the task that pupils are expected to carry out should be explained clearly and in terms of what the pupil has to do. The teacher's communication during any task in which the pupil is engaged should aid the pupils. Instructions should be clear and optimal and key words should be explained. The teacher may ensure that her own language is helpful by asking a colleague to observe a lesson or part of a lesson and comment on the effectiveness of the teacher's communication. Good teacher communication is likely also to help the pupil develop better attention skills. This includes the teacher breaking instructions into simple steps, either verbally or by using pictures or written support to help structure the activity (Thompson, 2003, p. 58). The notion of the teacher as a reflective practitioner is relevant here. Where a pupil is not responding to a request or suggestion or does not appear to understand the teacher, the teacher's first thought could helpfully be, not 'Why is the child ignoring me/being unco-operative?', but 'What did I not make clear?'

Allowing the pupil time to respond

The teacher may allow pupils who have difficulty with comprehension extra time to respond to questions. In whole-class teaching, this can be done in a way that does not compromise the pace of the lesson if a longer time is allowed for all pupils to answer some questions, because they are open questions or because they are difficult. A pupil with difficulties in comprehension can be selected to answer some more straightforward questions and a slightly longer waiting time will not then be as noticeable, because other pupils will have taken a while before responding to their questions. Naturally, in relation to the whole class the teacher will balance questions taking longer with easy, closed questions that are answered quickly to keep the pace of the lesson brisk overall.

In small-group work, a pupil with difficulties in comprehension can more easily be allowed more time to answer. In individual one-to-one work with an LSA, this strategy is also helpful. Pre-tutoring can be used to prepare the pupil for what is to come, so that his response times are likely to be shorter. Follow-up teaching to check, reinforce and further develop comprehension is also beneficial.

Support for the particular language demands of different school subjects

For some pupils, comprehension difficulties may be exacerbated by the specific demands of particular subjects. For example, history by definition will often deal with matters that are not in the present and this aspect can cause difficulties. Although information and activities can be supported by visual and other aids to understanding, such as time lines, the language may require clarification and perhaps some pre-learning of terms (depending on the pupil's age and his level of difficulty with comprehension), such as 'before', 'after' 'a century ago' and 'in the thirteenth century'.

A good approach, which can be formalised in school language policies, is for subject teachers to make a point of introducing new terms and allowing and encouraging some brief discussion of them to check comprehension. Such key words are often written in a prominent place by the teacher to remind pupils of the words and their spelling and this will also aid comprehension. All pupils will tend to be interested in understanding words that may be specific to the subject, as long as not too many are introduced at once. Therefore, in mathematics, interest can be generated from discussing the particular use of terms such as 'tables' (the matrix distinguished from the item of furniture), 'even' (as in even numbers distinguished from a level surface) and 'odd' (as in odd numbers discriminated from something that is peculiar).

Of course, care is needed to present terms and to check the pupils' understanding of vocabulary that tends to be used only in certain subjects, such as in geography, where 'oxbow lake', 'tributary', 'sedimentation' and so on might be used. Discussion, checking by the teacher questioning pupils and written exercises with an element of comprehension all contribute. With pupils having difficulties with comprehension, such features of good teaching may need to be repeated and reinforced, perhaps in small groups or with an LSA.

THINKING POINTS

Readers may wish to consider:

◆ the procedures the school has for ensuring that a child's difficulties with comprehension are detected early and are not misinterpreted as poor behaviour;
◆ the extent to which the teacher's own communication might be improved to help all pupils understand the learning points of the lesson and what is expected of each pupil;
◆ the effectiveness of the teacher's ways of checking the comprehension of all pupils, including those having difficulties with comprehension, for example through pupils signalling when they do not understand.

KEY TEXT

Bishop, D. V. M. (1997) *Uncommon Understanding: Development and Disorders of Language Comprehension in Children*, Hove, Psychology Press.

This book conveys some of the complexities involved in comprehending language. Its chapter headings give a flavour of what is covered: 'From sound to meaning: a framework for analysing comprehension', 'Specific language impairment', 'Speech perception', 'Understanding word meaning', 'Grammatical knowledge in sentence comprehension', 'Understanding sentences in real time', 'Understanding discourse: integrating language and context', 'Understanding intended meaning: social aspects of comprehension' and 'Modularity and interaction in language and development disorders'. (Modularity concerns the view that many processes involved in comprehension are undertaken by special brain systems known as 'modules'.)

Chapter 7

Provision for pupils with autistic spectrum disorders

INTRODUCTION

This chapter seeks to define autism and ASD. The triad of impairments associated with autism – social isolation, communication difficulties and insistence on sameness – is explained, along with how these impairments interact and affect learning. I consider the causes, prevalence and identification and assessment of ASD.

I explain various interventions: 'structured teaching' (ST), the Lovaas programme, intensive interaction, musical interaction therapy, signing systems for communication, the PECS, managing challenging behaviour if it occurs, working in pairs and groups, managing transitions, social stories, adults learning to use speech optimally and affective cognition.

Autism

Leo Kanner, an American psychiatrist, wrote a description of several children attending his psychiatric unit, delineating their limited interest in other people, odd language, insistence on routines and repetitive behaviour (Kanner, 1943). In doing so, he used the Greek word 'autism' to convey their apparent self-absorption, although the term 'Kanner syndrome' was used for some time afterwards as an alternative and still persists, as does the expression 'classical autism' (e.g. DfES/DoH, 2001a, p. 19). Later definitions have centred around a 'triad' of impairments (Wing and Gould, 1979), which concerns social isolation, communication difficulties and insistence on sameness.

The American Psychiatric Association classification system used by the *Diagnostic and Statistical Manual of Mental Disorders – Fourth Edition, Text Revision DSM-IV-TR Revision* (American Psychiatric Association, 2000) defines autism in terms of social difficulties, communication impairment and restricted behaviours. All three deficits must be present, with the social deficit being particularly marked.

The diagnostic criteria relating to social interaction (of which at least two of the elements must be manifested) are:

- marked impairment in the use of multiple non-verbal behaviours . . . ;
- failure to develop peer relationships appropriate to developmental level;
- a lack of spontaneous seeking to share enjoyment, interests, or achievement with other people . . . ;
- lack of emotional reciprocity.

(p. 75)

It has been estimated that between a third and a half of autistic children do not develop speech (Prizant and Wetherby, 1993) and require teaching alternative ways of communicating such as signing (see section on p. 81). Regarding communication and language, Jones (2002) suggests that a pupil with ASD:

- may not understand the purpose of communication;
- may initiate very little communication with others;
- may not show or share an interest with others;
- may be delayed in learning to speak or speech may not develop at all;
- may make limited or inappropriate use of gesture, eye contact, facial expression or body language;
- may have a good vocabulary and speak fluently but not communicate effectively;
- may talk at, rather than with, the person;
- may have problems in the social timing of communications.

(pp. 3–4)

Turning to thinking and behaving flexibly, the pupil with ASD shows 'restricted repetitive and stereotyped patterns of behaviour, interests and activities' (American Psychiatric Association, 2000, p. 75). He may spend much time and energy on a particular interest, may have little imaginative or symbolic play and may also play in an unusual way. He may be resistant to changes in routine, and may engage in repetitive activities.

With reference to sensory perception and responses, adults with ASD have reported being particularly sensitive to certain sounds (e.g. Lawson, 1998), while some children with Asperger's syndrome seem under-sensitive to certain stimuli.

Autistic spectrum disorders

Since the 1990s, the term 'autistic spectrum disorders' (ASD) (suggested by psychiatrist Lorna Wing, 1996) has come to be used to indicate autism and several other conditions thought to share certain important similarities. As well as autism, ASD include the following conditions:

- Pervasive development disorder. Not otherwise specified
- Asperger's syndrome
- Rett's syndrome
- Childhood disintegrative disorder
- Semantic–pragmatic disorder
- Schizoid personality disorder.

Pervasive developmental disorder includes the spectrum of autism and atypical autistic disorders. 'Pervasive development disorder. Not otherwise specified' (PDD.NOS) is also called atypical autism and is sometimes regarded as a milder form of autism; for example, a child with PDD.NOS may have impairments in either communication disorders or insistence on sameness/restricted behaviour but not necessarily both.

Asperger's syndrome takes its name from Hans Asperger, an Austrian paediatrician who described behaviours that have come to define the syndrome. It is sometimes viewed as a form of autism in which the child has an intelligence quotient within the normal range, but its assessment, unlike autism, does not require that the child experiences a communication deficit in the same way. Because the features of Asperger's syndrome may not be as marked as those of typical autism, they may not be noticed as early. Practical suggestions in relation to Asperger's syndrome may be found in Cumine *et al.* (2000).

Rett's syndrome affects girls only and usually becomes evident after a period of normal development of about six months. Skills in social interaction deteriorate. The brain does not continue to develop at its normal rate of growth, and cognitive, motor and speech skills are impaired. A typical feature is the persistent wringing or clapping of the hands. The girl usually has severe learning difficulties. For further information, see Lewis and Wilson (1998).

Childhood disintegrative disorder becomes evident after a period of normal development of about two years or longer. The child's skills deteriorate and there are cognitive, motor and social impairments. The condition affects boys more frequently than girls.

Semantic–pragmatic disorder is a developmental disorder concerning language meaning and function (see also Chapter 5: 'Difficulties in the use of language'). The child speaking fluently, with well-formed utterances and adequate articulation, typifies it, but the content of the language may be bizarre and the child may be echolalic or use over-learned 'scripts'. He may produce utterances without appearing to understand them. The child may interpret the language of another too literally or may respond to one or two words in an utterance. In conversation, the child has problems turn-taking and keeping to a topic. Some authors regard semantic–pragmatic disorder as a condition separate from ASD, but others have argued that it should be considered as part of ASD. One study (Gagnon *et al.*, 1997) found that a great majority of children assessed as having semantic–pragmatic disorder in the UK also fitted the criteria for ASD and that so few did not that it did not seem reasonable to continue a separate diagnostic category.

Schizoid personality disorder has been defined as a 'pervasive pattern of detachment from social relationships and a restricted range of expression and emotions in interpersonal settings' (American Psychiatric Association, 2000, p. 694). The condition is considered to differ from ASD in that, for example, a person with schizoid personality disorder tends to have less severe problems in personal relationships and they emerge in later childhood or adulthood rather than in early childhood. However, it is argued that there is a case for considering schizoid personality within ASD (Wolff, 1998).

Children with ASD range in intelligence from pupils considered to have profound learning difficulties, to pupils of above average ability. Particular approaches are considered necessary for pupils with ASD who have severe or profound learning difficulties. The age of onset of ASD for most children is within the first three years of life.

About a third of children with ASD, it has been estimated, have epilepsy (Volkmar and Nelson, 1990). The ratio of males to females identified with ASD is about 4:1 or 5:1 where there are other learning difficulties (Lord and Schopler, 1987). The ratio of males to females in higher ability groups with ASD may be as high as 10:1. Children from ethnic minorities appear to be 'under-represented' in referrals for diagnosis (Jones, 2002, p. 10).

Causes of ASD

There is considered to be 'overwhelming evidence' that autism has a biological basis and a strong genetic component (Medical Research Council, 2001, p. 21). ASD are believed to have several causes, perhaps all affecting the same brain systems. Several genes may act with environmental factors to lead to ASD but the precise genes are not yet known (e.g. Rutter, 1996). Among possible environmental factors are:

◆ illness during pregnancy
◆ childhood illness
◆ food intolerance
◆ reaction to vaccines and pollutants.

It will be obvious, however, that children experience these environmental factors without developing ASD, so it is the interaction between such possible factors and proposed genetic and biological factors that appears to be influential. Among psychological theories seeking to explain characteristics of ASD is the notion that people with ASD do not have a sufficiently developed 'theory of mind' and experience particular difficulties in recognising and interpreting the emotional and mental states of others, leading to social and communication difficulties (e.g. Baron-Cohen, 2000).

Prevalence of ASD

Prevalence in relation to SEN refers to the number of children with a particular type of SEN in a specified population over a specified period. Incidence is usually expressed as the number of children per live births in a given year. Prevalence relates to incidence in the sense that prevalence is determined by the incidence of a condition and its duration (see also Farrell, 2003, pp. 129–30).

Establishing the prevalence of ASD is fraught with difficulties, including lack of agreement about the list of conditions that should be included within the range of ASD, the qualitative nature of the definitions and diagnostic criteria, and the lack of agreement about which professional body or group might be best placed (and informed) to identify the condition. A recent estimate (Medical Research Council, 2001) indicates that ASD affect approximately 60 in every 10,000 children under the age of 8 years. Classic autism is estimated to affect 10 to 30 children per 10,000, although the rate for the population that includes older children and adults may be higher.

Regarding 'autistic spectrum disorder', in January 2004 in England (DfES, 2004, table 9), there were 7,300 pupils at School Action Plus representing 2.1 per cent of pupils at this part of the SEN framework and a further 23,960 pupils with statements of SEN or 10.1 per cent of pupils with statements.

The specific figures for ordinary primary and secondary schools and for special schools are as follows. In primary schools, 5,330 of pupils with ASD were at School Action Plus (2.4 per cent of all pupils at School Action Plus in primary schools) and 10,610 had statements of SEN (15.4 per cent of all pupils with statements in primary schools). In secondary schools, the number was smaller, being 1,800 at School Action Plus (1.4 per cent) and 4,900 with statements of SEN (6.2 per cent). In special schools, where it is much less usual for pupils not to have statements of SEN, there were only 160 pupils at School Action Plus (10 per cent) and 8,450 with statements of SEN (9.5 per cent). The figures for special schools included pupils attending maintained and non-maintained special schools but excluded pupils in independent special schools and pupils in maintained hospital schools.

Identification and assessment of ASD

Early identification and intervention are important. The identification ('diagnosis') of ASD may be undertaken by a paediatrician, psychiatrist, educational psychologist, clinical psychologist, SALT or a general practitioner. A multi-disciplinary assessment may be carried out, drawing together the perspectives of the teachers, parents, educational psychologist, SALT and others. Some LEAs have designated particular professionals with specialist knowledge and experience of children with ASD.

Among initial broad screening instruments are:

◆ The *Checklist for Autism in Toddlers (CHAT)* (Baron-Cohen *et al.*, 1992)

The *CHAT* may be used by general practitioners or health visitors when the child's development is routinely assessed. It consists of questions for parents and a series of situations that are created so that the child's response can be observed. If it appears that the child may have autism, further assessment is required.

◆ The *Gilliam Autism Rating Scale (GARS)* (Gilliam, 1995)

The *GARS*, which is used with children and young people aged 4 to 20 years, comprises items based on the definitions of autism used by the *DSM-IV-TR* and elsewhere. The three core subtests are stereotyped behaviours, communication and social interaction. It is used by SALTs, educational psychologists, SENCOs and specialist teachers.

For a thorough diagnosis to be made, it is necessary to combine systematic observations of the child at home (and/or in other settings), and an account of the child's history from birth to the present. Diagnostic instruments have been developed using interviews, ratings and structured observations, for example the

Diagnostic Interview for Social and Communication Disorders (Wing *et al.*, 2002). Further sources of information for diagnostic assessment include information from the child as appropriate, the child's parents and other members of the family and discussions with professionals who know the child well (e.g. DfES/DoH, 2001a, p. 9, section 2.9). Discussions are required about how and when the diagnosis of ASD is conveyed to the parent, the child and other family members.

Among forms of assessment used with children having ASD, is the *Vineland Adaptive Behaviour Scale* (Sparrow *et al.*, 1984) for which norms have been calculated for use with children with ASD (Carter *et al.*, 1998). It collates information from parents or key workers in the developmental areas of socialisation, communication, daily living skills and motor skills. Pupil self-assessment can be helpful, perhaps using a checklist of self-descriptive statements (Parker, 2000).

Some assessments seek to identify Asperger's syndrome as a distinct condition. These include the following:

◆ *Gilliam Asperger's Disorder Scale* (*GADS*) (Gilliam, 2000)

The *GADS* is intended for an age range of 3 to 22 years and has 32 items divided into 4 subscales describing measurable behaviours.

◆ *Asperger's Syndrome Diagnostic Scale* (*ASDS*) (Myles *et al.*, 2000b)

This scale is intended for 5 to 18-year-olds and comprises 50 'yes/no' items concerning the areas: cognitive, maladaptive, language, social and sensori-motor.

Provision

Professional standards

The *National Special Educational Needs Specialist Standards* (Teacher Training Agency, 1999) set out standards concerning the effective teaching of pupils having severe and/or complex needs (p. 1). These are intended as an auditing aid to help head teachers and teachers identify training and development needs. They are structured as core standards, extension standards, standards in relation to key SEN roles and responsibilities, and skills and attributes. The 'extension standards' give an indication of the knowledge and understanding and the skills associated with teaching children with ASD.

Teachers with additional specialist skills should know and understand:

i.   the characteristics of autistic spectrum disorder and their implications for communication and learning;
ii. the range of individual differences within the autistic spectrum disorder;
iii. the impact of the co-occurrence of different types of difficulty e.g. *dyspraxia and an autistic spectrum disorder*;

(p. 16, italics in original)

i.   the likely reasons for challenging behaviour in autistic spectrum disorder, including passivity as well as apparently aggressive behaviours.

(p. 22)

Teachers with additional specialist skills should demonstrate skills in:

    i.   teaching pupils to accept, initiate and maintain relationships with others, and how to communicate in social contexts;

(p. 17)

    i.   identify[ing] the effects of autistic spectrum disorder on learning styles;
    ii. devising and implementing individual and group programmes which help pupils to learn in social contexts, which foster attention to the task;

(p. 20)

    1   develop[ing] flexible thinking and behaviour and modifying and using pupils' obsessional interests or behaviour.

(p. 23)

'Structured teaching'

Division TEACCH (Treatment and Education of Autistic and related Communication handicapped CHildren) is a programme in the state of North Carolina, USA for people with ASD and their families. One aspect of its work has been the development of ST, an approach 'designed to address the major neurological differences in autism' (Mesibov and Howley, 2003, p. 8). It seeks to address difficulties with receptive language, expressive communication, working memory problems, attending relevantly, organisation, dealing with other people and sensory stimulation (overreaction to stimulation in the environment).

ST involves organising the classroom and ensuring that the teaching process and teaching styles are suitable for pupils with ASD. Visual information is used to make things more meaningful and to encourage learning and independence. The main purpose of ST is to 'increase independence and to manage behaviour by considering the cognitive skills, needs and interests of people with ASD and adjusting the environment accordingly' (p. 9). Four components of ST (which may be used flexibly to help access to the National Curriculum) are physical structure, daily schedules, work systems, and visual structure and information.

Physical structure and organisation concerns 'the way of arranging the furniture, materials and general surroundings to add meaning and context to the environment' (p. 26). It may include such features as providing the child with a work-station, screening an area to reduce distractions, and using different colours to designate a room or area for different activities.

Daily schedules involve such features as visual timetables and diaries, either written or using pictures and drawings or representative objects to help the pupil organise moving from place to place and from activity to activity. For example, a transition object can be presented to a child to indicate what he should do next (e.g. a picture of a coat to indicate going outside for break-time). A simple sequence can be indicated by trays labelled 'first' and 'then', which contain items necessary for two different tasks. Alternatives offered in schedules can encourage pupils' choice and decision-making.

Work systems, presented visually, aim to aid the pupil in completing specific activities. The work system may be organised to go from left to right so that, for example, work concerning specific tasks and activities is placed in a tray on the pupil's left and, as work is completed, it is transferred to a 'finished' tray on the right. For higher-attaining pupils, work systems can be written.

Visual structure and information concerning specific tasks and activities includes ensuring organisation and structures using the principles of visual clarity (e.g. colour coding), visual organisation (e.g. using organising containers) and visual instructions (e.g. written or pictorial cues).

Lovaas programme

The Lovaas programme, sometimes called applied behaviour analysis, uses behavioural methods to teach skills and reduce unwanted behaviour (Lovaas, 1987). For an outline of the behavioural perspective within the context of behavioural, emotional and social difficulties, see the book in this series, *The Effective Teacher's Guide to Behavioural Emotional and Social Difficulties: Practical Strategies*, Chapter 4: 'Behavioural approach'.

In the Lovaas programme, some behaviours are considered to be in excess, such as obsessive behaviour, while others are considered to be in deficit, such as communication and social skills. The aim, therefore, is to decrease excess behaviours and develop and increase deficit behaviours.

Usually, the child is taught at home, one-to-one, by a therapist who is trained to use the programme, and by the child's parents and volunteers. It is recommended that, ideally, the programme should begin before the child is 42 months old. Teaching takes place in 10–15-minute sessions, followed by a period of play, followed by a further session of work. Normally, the child sits opposite the therapist at a table and instructions are given with physical prompts as necessary. Required responses are rewarded while unwanted responses are ignored or given time out.

Target behaviours are specified (e.g. repeating a word) and a sequence or 'drill' is presented to teach the target behaviour. The first three goals, 'come here', 'sit down' and 'look at me', are followed by work such as imitation, matching, labelling objects and pre-school academic skills.

To the extent that the Lovaas programme is considered effective and to the degree that it follows behavioural principles, more general behavioural approaches used in school with pupils having ASD can be expected to lead to progress.

Intensive interaction

A principle of intensive interaction (e.g. Hewett and Nind, 1998) is that it is necessary to develop the child's ability to enjoy the company of others, and to develop his understanding of how to interact with others and how to communicate. It uses techniques relating to early parent–child interactions, in which the earliest possible random actions of the child are invested with meaning by the parent through imitation and turn-taking. In intensive interaction, then, the adult acts as though the actions of the child were intended to communicate meaning and follows what the child does.

Short daily interactions in the classroom aim to develop communication and encourage learning, so that the developing relationship leads to other activities within a wider curriculum. Parents who have been trained can also use the approach at home. The progress of pupils using this approach have been assessed and reported (Nind, 1999).

Musical interaction therapy

As with intensive interaction, musical interaction therapy (e.g. Prevezer, 2000) seeks to develop the child's ability to enjoy the company of others and his under-standing of how to interact and communicate. Research evidence to support its use is reported by Wimpory and colleagues (1995). Normal communication is seen as developing as the baby and the familiar adult negotiate increasingly complex inter-actions in which the baby actively participates. The interaction takes place as the baby responds to the adult and invites a response so that a dialogue develops.

Building on this rationale, musical interaction therapy involves the child's parent or a key worker working with the child having ASD, while a musician plays an instrument to support and encourage their interaction. For example, the key worker might copy or join in with the child's actions as if they were intentional attempts to communicate.

Signing systems for communication

Manual sign systems, using hand and arm positioning and movements to communi-cate, include Makaton (Walker, 1980, 1993 and see address list in this volume) and Signalong (see address list). Makaton is a language programme offering a basic means of communicating and can be used to encourage the development of verbal language skills. The Makaton Vocabulary Development Project has a national network of regional and local tutors who train and advise parents, teachers, SALTs and others to use Makaton. Publications include books of signs and symbols, videos and computer databases. Signalong is a sign-supporting system that is based on BSL and is used with pupils with learning difficulties and autism. Training and advice is provided by Signalong staff and by accredited tutors. Publications include manuals with signing instructions and Signalong works with other organisations to develop symbols to allow wider communication.

Signing systems might be expected to be effective as a communication tool for pupils with ASD, for example because they are visual and the child's hand movements when he is signing can be modified and corrected by an adult. Yet many children with ASD appear to have difficulties in making signs and using them spontaneously (Attwood *et al.*, 1988). It is thought to be more effective to use signing to help a child's understanding rather than to teach it to be used as a means of expression (Jones, 2002, p. 59). For example, adults can use signing when speaking to a child to give an extra physical clue to what is being communicated.

The Picture Exchange Communication System

The PECS (Bondy and Frost, 1994) aims to help children, using pictures, to request things or activities from others (www.pecs.org.uk). The child 'exchanges' a picture or a symbol representing, for example, an item or activity for the thing they would like. Single things are taught initially, such as 'drink'. It is important in early stages not to pre-empt the child's attempts to communicate by volunteering the communication that is anticipated, but to wait for the child to hand over the picture conveying the request. Later, further to develop communication, the child is taught to construct sentences and to use pictures to offer comments.

Managing challenging behaviour if it occurs

Challenging behaviour is not a necessary concomitant of ASD, but, where it does occur, the context of ASD can be influential in its prevention and management. Important considerations are the environment in which challenging behaviour occurs, what appears to precipitate it, the challenging behaviour itself, and the responses it elicits – all principles of behavioural approaches.

It is from these considerations that strategies are developed to prevent and/ or manage challenging behaviour. The environment may be modified (cf. 'Structured teaching', pp. 79–80) or what is requested of the child may be refined (e.g. obsessional behaviour is not disallowed but, providing it is harmless, allowed in recreation periods after school activities and tasks are completed). Also, it is conveyed to the child that certain behaviour is not acceptable (cf. aspects of the Lovaas programme, p. 80, which seeks to reduce behaviours that are considered to be in excess). Learning the consequences of actions can be aided by the use of communication aids and alternatives (e.g. PECS). (See also, Whitaker, 2001.)

Working in pairs and groups

While social situations tend to be difficult for pupils with ASD, much is learned in pairs and small groups in school. Strategies for encouraging group work therefore reflect a tension requiring the sensitivity of the teacher.

Working on a principle related to desensitisation in behavioural approaches, the pupil with ASD can be first taught individually by the teacher or an LSA but in successively closer proximity to a small group of other pupils. The pupil can then work with one other child on an activity with which the child with ASD is familiar so that the child's efforts at adapting are largely on the social aspects of the activity. Both the task and the level of social interaction required can be gradually increased in complexity. Next, the pupil could be encouraged to work in a group of three pupils where again the task and social requirements can be gradually increased. Larger-group work would follow. Balanced against such gradual development of tolerance and skill development within group work is the importance for the child with ASD of also having some time alone and/or pursuing a preferred activity.

Managing transitions

Teachers need to be aware of the stress that can be brought about at times of transition for any child, whether this involves starting school, moving to another school or experiencing changes at home. Because of the nature of ASD, transition needs to be managed sensitively as changes in routine are often particularly difficult for the child. Major transitions such as the change from primary to secondary school and the move from school to further or higher education or employment (Jones, 2002, pp. 104–14) require careful support (e.g. DfES/DoH, 2001a, p. 16). Aids to successful transition include good LEA policies and procedures for transition, effective record-keeping, good preparation for transfer, strong support from Connexions personal advisers, and careful monitoring of the success of the transitions (DfES/DoH, 2001b, pp. 110–21).

Social stories

Much attention has been given to the use of social stories with pupils with ASD. The stories are intended to help pupils understand the social environment and to know how to behave suitably in it, focusing on a desired outcome. As originally conceived (Gray, 1994), social stories are written by someone who knows the pupil well and concern a social situation that the pupil finds difficult. The format includes descriptive, perspective and directive sentences. Descriptive sentences concern what happens, where it happens, who participates, what they do and why they do it. Perspective sentences describe the feelings and responses of others. Directive sentences tend to give guidance rather than commands and concern what the pupil should try to do or say in the situation (e.g. 'I should try to . . .'). It is suggested that a social story has proportionately more descriptive and perspective statements than directive statements.

The pupil may write and develop his own stories focused on matters and situations that he might find difficult (e.g. Smith, 2003). The discussion centring on the developing story and the anticipation of the real-life situation they describe may be important components. As well as written social stories, a comic strip format can be used with characters having speech bubbles and thought bubbles to convey similar information and guidance to that of written stories. Photographs and symbols can be employed. More information needs to be gathered on what social stories are intended to achieve, whether they achieve it, which pupils tend to benefit and how long-lasting any effects are on a child's behaviour and well-being.

Adults learning to use speech optimally

The point of adults seeking to use an optimal amount and type of speech is to find a level that will facilitate a child's understanding. In practice, this often means using less speech and adopting key words. It is not the intention that the adult's speech becomes robotic or painfully stilted. If this were so, the model of speech for the pupil to hear would be impoverished. What is ideally sought is that the teacher or other adult develops an awareness that too much and too complicated speech tends only to confuse and frustrate the child. It is this awareness that leads to speech being more selective and, where necessary, being characterised by emphasising key meaning words.

Affective cognition

In the approach called 'affective cognition', ASD is considered to lead to 'difficulties in mapping causal connections from the child's own feelings to their thoughts and from an experience of self to the perception of equivalence in the behaviours of others' (Sherratt and Donald, 2004, p. 10). Children with ASD are regarded as having difficulty in perceiving as relevant aspects of experience that are deemed significant by others, and have difficulty in developing a shared understanding of the world. This is taken to account for the limited social engagement and limited 'connectedness' of children with ASD and many other typical features of autism, for example that children with ASD tend to perceive items and events untypically and develop responses to them that are idiosyncratic.

Affective cognition involves the use of teaching structures for encouraging progress in social engagement. It has been described as 'a teaching approach that attempts to build shared understanding of self, others and the environment by engaging within a mutually meaningful process' (p. 11). Also, it 'builds episodes of social engagement between the child with autism and another' (p. 12). It aims to develop 'connectedness' through interactive processes that are meaningful and that are 'anchored around the child's saliencies' (that is, what processes and objects are prominent, important, attractive and exciting for the child). This, it is maintained, leads to 'more effective sociocultural learning', which helps the development of more complex 'narratives' (a sequence of meanings and intentions that hold together) and these are the foundation of what becomes an understanding of other people's thoughts, desires, beliefs and so on (p. 10).

Affective cognition involves ten teaching structures that encourage early social engagement, a shared understanding of objects and processes, and a shared understanding of symbolic representation in play and language. The structures are: 'establishing engagement around primary social saliencies' (for example, using repetitive movements or chasing games as the medium through which connectedness is established); 'establishing engagement around social sequences and processes and beginning to incorporate songs and rhymes within the process'; 'using objects to establish shared meanings about a process' (for example, functional activities later leading to introducing different ways in which an object might be used); 'developing shared understanding of simple narratives'; 'developing shared understanding around an established narrative'; 'developing a shared understanding of symbols within play'; 'developing more complex narratives using language and symbolic play'; 'developing simple conversational sequences using language'; 'developing abstract, imaginative and fantasy ideas and using these as a focus of the interaction'; and 'developing extended narratives using abstract mental state ideas and open ended questions' (p. 14).

THINKING POINTS

Readers may wish to consider:

◆ how secure and agreed are locally used definitions of ASD and related systems of identification and assessment;
◆ the range of interventions available locally and how their effectiveness or otherwise is monitored.

KEY TEXTS

Department for Education and Skills and Department of Health (2001a) *Autistic Spectrum Disorders: Good Practice Guidance – 01 Guidance on Autistic Spectrum Disorders*, London, DfES/DoH.

This booklet sets out to answer several of the often asked questions about ASD and has a useful glossary and appendices of publications and addresses.

———————

Department for Education and Skills and Department of Health (2001b) *Autistic Spectrum Disorders: Good Practice Guidance – 02 Pointers to Good Practice*, London, DfES/DoH.

This booklet includes 'pointers' concerning advocacy, early years, family support and short breaks, funding, home-based provision, identification, information and communications technology, in-service training, LEA outreach support services, LEA policy, mainstream or special school placement decisions, multi-agency support, regional co-ordination, school provision for children with ASD, speech and language therapy and transition.

———————

Jones, G. (2002) *Educational Provision for Children with Autism and Asperger's Syndrome: Meeting Their Needs*, London, David Fulton Publishers.

This book gives a compact yet sensitive overview of ASD, their identification, assessment relating to teaching and behaviour management, and educational interventions. It comments on the life of people with ASD after school, for example in further and higher education and in employment.

———————

Chapter 8

Conclusion

Outline

The *Special Educational Needs Code of Practice* (DfES, 2001) forms a starting point for examining the broad area of communication and interaction difficulties and its possible relationship with other areas of SEN. The triggers for intervention at Early Years Action, Early Years Action Plus, School Action and School Action Plus and when a statement of SEN is issued are intended to form a graduated response. The guidance, *Data Collection by Type of Special Educational Needs* (DfES, 2003) provides brief descriptions of 'speech, language and communication needs' and 'autistic spectrum disorder'. Such definitions and descriptions of speech and language difficulties can be related to the layered legal definition of SEN in the Education Act 1996 and further understood in that context, although ASD is less well illuminated by the layered definition. The *Code* (DfES, 2001) touches on the type of provision that pupils with communication and interaction difficulties 'may require' (7: 56). In this book I have stressed the importance of having a range of provision including mainstream schools and special schools for pupils and have also underlined the importance of professionals working together and of schools working with parents and seeking their involvement and of involving pupils.

Provision for pupils with speech difficulties may involve individual programmes and use communication other than speech. Educating pupils with grammar difficulties involves ensuring that the teacher's communication is clear and interventions include encouraging pupils' interest in grammatical features of utterances and shaping pupils' responses. Semantic problems are helped by improving labelling skills, packaging and networking and by other means. Responses to pragmatic difficulties include strategies to improve conversational skills. Comprehension problems are helped by aiding attention, teaching listening behaviour and other approaches. In all approaches, close liaison between the teacher, the SALT and others is important.

Although, for ease of explanation, difficulties with speech, grammar, semantics, pragmatics and comprehension have largely been presented separately, they do not exist in isolation but, as has been indicated in earlier chapters, interrelate. Difficulties that make speech barely intelligible may hide difficulties with other areas such as semantics. Similarly, with ASD, the triad of impairments involving social isolation, communication difficulties and insistence of sameness interrelate and compound the pupil's difficulties. Social isolation and insistence on sameness, for example, reduce opportunities for communication.

Many interventions have been indicated and the particular blend of approaches will be suggested by a careful assessment of the child and his situation and rigorous programme-planning, the results of which should be monitored and evaluated.

Other ways of outlining difficulties with communication

In this book, the structure has been to consider various aspects of communication and communication difficulties in terms of speech (phonology, phonetics and prosody), grammar (syntax and morphology), meaning (semantics and vocabulary), pragmatics and comprehension.

Other ways of considering the area of communication and associated difficulties are used elsewhere and include, for example, reference to receptive and expressive aspects of communication. Receptive aspects include the child's understanding of grammatical concepts and of conceptual language. On the other hand, expressive language concerns such features as the use of grammar and the use of vocabulary. The presentation adopted in this book will, however, enable the teacher to recognise the elements discussed in other formulations and, it is hoped, will provide a structure in which meaningful liaison can take place between the teacher, the SALT and others. Considering ASD separately reflects the differences between ASD and other difficulties with communication, including the difficulties with social understanding and inflexibility of thought and behaviour associated with the 'triad' of impairments.

Among other ways of reviewing information on communication and interaction difficulties are clinical perspectives. For example, Rapin and Allen (1987) provided a framework of clinical language subtypes, which, although it is perhaps not used as much as in the past, is of interest.

Another perspective is a psycholinguistic view of language (e.g. Stackhouse and Wells, 1997), which is important in seeking insight into, for example, phonological awareness or verbal dyspraxia. Among clinical language sub types are the following:

Verbal auditory agnosia

This is characterised by an inability to understand spoken language while the comprehension of gestures is unimpaired. The child either has no speech or speech is limited and typified by poor articulation.

Verbal dysphasia

The child understands adequately, but his speech is very limited, utterances being short and the production of speech sounds impaired. The child may have difficulty producing non-speech oral movements, but the difficulty in producing speech sounds cannot be accounted for by muscle weakness or neurologically related lack of co-ordination of articulators.

Phonological programming deficit syndrome

While the child's understanding is adequate, and he speaks fluently in fairly long utterances, his speech is hard to understand.

Phonologic–syntactic deficit syndrome

The child's speech is diffluent, utterances are short and he mispronounces words. Function words and grammatical inflections are omitted. The child finds difficulty understanding complex utterances and abstract language.

Lexical–syntactic deficit syndrome

The child produces speech sound normally but has difficulty with word-finding and in formulating connected language. Expressive syntax is immature. The child finds it harder to understand abstract language than to understand language about the here and now.

Semantic–pragmatic deficit syndrome

Semantic–pragmatic disorder, as mentioned in the previous chapter on ASD, is a developmental disorder concerning language meaning and function. The child speaking fluently with utterances being well formed and articulation being adequate typifies it. The content of the language may be bizarre, however, and the child may be echolalic or use over-learned 'scripts'. He may produce utterances without appearing to understand them. The child may interpret the language of others too literally or may respond to one or two words in an utterance. In conversation, the child has problems turn-taking and keeping to a topic.

The above clinical language subtypes are described in terms of the aspects of communication discussed in the present book (speech, grammar, meaning and use) and this should provide a point of entry for readers who wish to examine communication difficulties from a more clinical viewpoint.

Addresses

Association For All Speech Impaired Children
2nd Floor
50–2 Great Sutton Street
London EC1V 0DJ

Tel: 020 7490 9410
Helpline: 0845 355 5577
Fax: 020 7251 2834
e-mail: info@afasic.org.uk
www.afasic.org.uk

> AFASIC is a parent-led charity representing children and young adults having speech, language and communication impairments, working for their inclusion in society and supporting their parents and carers.

The Association of Educational Psychologists
26 The Avenue
Durham DH1 4ED

Tel: 0191 384 9512
Fax: 0191 386 5287
e-mail: aep@aep.org.uk
www.aep.org.uk

> The AEP is the professional association for educational psychologists in England and Wales and Northern Ireland.

The Association of Professional Music Therapists
61 Church Hill Road
East Barnet
Herts EN4 8SY

Tel/fax: 020 8440 4153
e-mail: APMToffice@aol.com
www.apmt.org

The APMT supports and develops the profession of music therapy. Its members are qualified music therapists who have taken a recognised post-graduate training course in music therapy. The association aims to maintain high standards of practice through administering and monitoring a range of professional development schemes.

British Psychological Society
St Andrew's House
48 Princess Road East
Leicester LE1 7DR

Tel: 0116 254 9568
Fax: 0116 247 0787
e-mail: bps1@le.ac.uk
www.bps.org.uk

The BPS is the professional body for psychologists in the UK, having various subgroups and divisions. It publishes monthly the magazine *Psychologist*, which is of generic interest to psychologists. Its specialist journals include *The British Journal of Clinical Psychology* and *The British Journal of Educational Psychology*.

The British Society for Music Therapy
61 Church Hill Road
East Barnet
Herts EN4 8SY

Tel: 020 8441 6226
Fax: 020 8441 4118
e-mail: info@bsmt.org
www.bsmt.org

The BSMT organises courses, conferences, workshops and meetings concerning music therapy which are open to all. An information booklet giving details of music therapy, training courses, books and meetings is available to enquirers. The BSMT has its own publications and offers music therapy books for sale. Members receive *The British Journal of Music Therapy* and the *BSMT Bulletin*.

Harcourt Assessment (The Psychological Corporation)
Halley Court, Jordan Hill
Oxford OX2 8EJ

Tel: 01865 888 188
Fax: 01865 314 348
e-mail: info@harcourt-uk.com
www.harcourt-uk.com

Harcourt Assessment are test suppliers whose assessments include ones relevant to speech and language difficulties and to autism.

I-CAN
4 Dyer's Buildings
London EC1N 2PQ

Tel: 0870 010 4066
Fax: 0870 010 4067
e-mail: ican@ican.org.uk
www.ican.org.uk

A national charity for children with speech and language difficulties.

Makaton Vocabulary Development Project
31 Firwood Drive
Camberley
Surrey GU15 3QD

Tel: 01276 61390
Fax: 01276 681368
e-mail: mvdp@makaton.org
www.makaton.org

National Autistic Society
393 City Road
London EC1V 1NG

Tel: 020 7833 2299
Fax: 020 7833 9666
e-mail: nas@nas.org.uk
www.nas.org.uk

The NAS runs schools and adult centres and works with LEAs to develop specialist services. It provides conferences and other forms of training and publications on autism. It supports local groups and families.

NFER-Nelson
The Chiswick Centre
414 Chiswick High Road
London W4 5TF

Tel: 020 8996 8444
Fax: 020 8996 5358
e-mail: edu&hsc@nfer-Nelson.co.uk
www.nfer-nelson.co.uk

NFER-Nelson are test suppliers whose tests include ones relevant to speech and language difficulties and autism.

Picture Exchange Communication System (PECS)
Pyramid Educational Consultants UK Ltd
Pavilion House, 6 Old Steine
Brighton BN1 1EJ

Tel: 01273 609 555
Fax: 01273 609 556
e-mail: pyramid@pecs.org.uk
www.pecs.org.uk

> Suppliers of the PECS programme teaching functional communication skills to those with communication difficulties.

The Royal College of Psychiatrists
17 Belgrave Square
London SW1X 8PG

Tel: 020 7235 2351
Fax: 020 7245 1231
e-mail: rcpsych@rcpsych.ac.uk
www.rcpsych.ac.uk

The Royal College of Speech and Language Therapists
2 White Hart Yard
London SE1 1NX

Tel: 020 7378 1200
Fax: 020 7403 7254
e-mail: postmaster@rcslt.org
www.rcslt.org

> The professional body for speech and language therapists in the UK, maintaining standards in ethical conduct, clinical practice and education of speech and language therapists.

The Signalong Group
Stratford House
Waterside Court, Neptune Way
Rochester
Kent ME2 4NZ

Tel: 0870 774 3752
www.signalong.org.uk

Widgit Software
124 Cambridge Science Park
Milton Road
Cambridge CB4 0ZS

Tel: 01223 425 558
Fax: 01223 425 349
e-mail: info@widgit.com
www.widgit.com

Bibliography

Adams, C., Coke, R., Crutchley, A. *et al.* (2001) *Assessment of Comprehension and Expression 6–11*, Windsor, NFER-Nelson.

Aitchison, J. (1994) *Words in the Mind*, Oxford, Blackwell.

Aitken, S. and Millar, S. (2002) *Listening to Children with Communication Support Needs*, Glasgow, Sense Scotland.

Aldred, C. *et al.* (2001) 'Multidisciplinary social communication intervention for children with autism and pervasive developmental disorder: the Child's Talk project', *Educational and Child Psychology* 18 (2): 76–87.

American Psychiatric Association (2000) *Diagnostic and Statistical Manual of Mental Disorders Fourth Edition, Text Revision (DSM-IV-TR)*, Washington, DC, American Psychiatric Association.

Anderson-Wood, L. and Smith, B. R. (1997) *Working with Pragmatics: A Practical Guide to Promoting Communicative Competence*, Bicester, Winslow Press.

Armstrong, S. and Ainley, M. (1988) *South Tyneside Assessment of Syntactic Structures*, South Tyneside, STASS Publications.

Asperger, H. (1944) 'Die "autistischen psychopathen" im *Kinder salter*', *Archiv für Psychiatrie Nervenkrankeiten* 117: 76–136; translation by Frith, U. (ed.) (1999) in *Autism and Asperger's Syndrome*, Cambridge, Cambridge University Press, pp. 37–92.

Association For All Speech Impaired Children (AFASIC) (1991) *AFASIC Checklists*, Wisbech, Language Development Aids.

Attwood *et al.* (1988) 'The understanding and use of interpersonal gestures by autistic and Down's syndrome children', *Journal of Autism and Developmental Disorders* 18: 241–57.

Baron-Cohen, S. (2000) *Understanding Others' Minds*, Oxford, Oxford University Press.

—— *et al.* (1992) 'Can autism be detected at 18 months? The needle, the haystack and the CHAT', *British Journal of Psychiatry* 161: 839–43.

Bishop, D. V. M. (1997) *Uncommon Understanding: Development and Disorders of Language Comprehension in Children*, Hove, Psychology Press.

—— (1998) 'Development of the children's communication checklist (CCC): a method for assessing qualitative aspects of communication impairment', *Journal of Child Psychology and Psychiatry* 39: 879–93.

Bondy, A. S. and Frost, L. A. (1994) 'The Picture Communication System', *Focus on Autistic Behaviour* 9 (3): 1–9.

Burnett, A. and Wylie, J. (2002) *Soundaround: Developing Phonological Awareness Skills in the Foundation Stage*, London, David Fulton Publishers.

Carter, A. S. *et al.* (1998) 'The Vineland Adaptive Behaviour Scale: supplementary norms for individuals with autism', *Journal of Autism and Developmental Disorders* 28: 287–302.

Crystal, D. (1976) *Language Assessment and Screening Procedure* (*LARSP*), New York, Elsevier.

Cumine, V., Leach, J. and Stevenson, G. (2000) *Asperger's Syndrome: A Practical Guide for Teachers*, London, David Fulton Publishers.

Dean, E., Howell, J. and Waters, D. (1990) *Metaphon Resource Pack*, Windsor, NFER-Nelson.

Department for Education and Employment/Qualifications and Curriculum Authority (1999a) *The National Curriculum Handbook for Primary Teachers in England Key Stages 1 and 2*, London, DfEE/QCA.

—— (1999b) *The National Curriculum Handbook for Secondary Teachers in England Key Stages 3 and 4*, London, DfEE/QCA.

Department for Education and Skills (2001) *Special Educational Needs Code of Practice*, London, DfES.

—— (2003) *Data Collection by Type of Special Educational Needs*, London, DfES.

—— (2004) *National Statistics First Release: Special Educational Needs in England, January 2004 (SFR 44/2004)*, London, DfES.

Department for Education and Skills and Department of Health (2001a) *Autistic Spectrum Disorder Good Practice Guidance: 01 Guidance on Autistic Spectrum Disorders*, London, DfES.

—— and —— (2001b) *Autistic Spectrum Disorder Good Practice Guidance: 02 Pointers to Good Practice*, London, DfES.

Dewart, H. and Summers, S. (1995) *The Pragmatic Profile of Everyday Communication Skills in School Aged Children*, Windsor, NFER-Nelson.

Dodd, B., Crosbie, S., McIntosh, B. *et al.* (2000) *Preschool and Primary Inventory of Phonological Awareness*, London, Harcourt Assessment.

Dunn, Lloyd M., Dunn, Leota M., Whetton, C. *et al.* (1997) *British Picture Vocabulary Scale*, Windsor, NFER-Nelson.

Edwards, S., Fletcher, P., Garman, M. *et al.* (1997) *Reynell Developmental Language Scales*, Windsor, NFER-Nelson.

Farrell, M. (2003) *Special Education Handbook* (3rd edn), London, David Fulton Publishers.

Foster, S. H. (1990) *The Communicative Competence of Young Children: A Modular Approach*, New York, Longman.

Gagnon, L., Mottron, L. and Jonette, Y. (1997) 'Questioning the validity of the Semantic–Pragmatic Syndrome diagnosis', *Autism* 1: 37–55.

German, D. J. (1986) *National College of Education Test of Word Finding*, Allen, TX: DLM Teaching Resources.

Gilliam, J. E. (1995) *Gilliam Autism Rating Scale* (G*ARS*), Windsor, NFER-Nelson.

—— (2000) *Gilliam Aspergers Disorder Scale* (*GADS*), Oxford, Harcourt Assessment.

Gray, C. (1994) *The Social Story Book*, Arlington, TX, Future Horizons.

Hagues, N., Siddiqui, R. and Merwood, P. (1999) *Listening Comprehension Test Series*, Windsor, NFER-Nelson.

Hammill, D. D. and Newcomer, P. L. (1997) *Test of Language Development – Intermediate, Third Edition* (*TOLD-I:3*), Oxford, The Psychological Corporation.

——, Brown, V. L., Larsen, C. and Wiederholt, J. L. (1994) *Test of Adolescent and Adult Language, Third Edition* (*TOAL–3*), Oxford, The Psychological Corporation.

Hewett, D. and Nind, M. (1998) *Interaction in Action*, London, David Fulton Publishers.

Hornby, G. (2003) 'Counselling and guidance of parents' in Hornby, G., Hall, C. and Hall, E. *Counselling Pupils in Schools: Skills and Strategies for Teachers* (2nd edn), London, RoutledgeFalmer, pp. 129–40.

Howell, J. and Dean, E. (1994) *Treating Phonological Disorders in Children: Metaphon – Theory to Practice*, London, Whurr.

I-CAN (2001) *Joint Professional Development Framework*, London, I-CAN.

Jones, G. (2002) *Educational Provision for Children with Autism and Asperger's Syndrome: Meeting Their Needs*, London, David Fulton Publishers.

Jordan, R. (2001) *Autism with Severe Learning Difficulties*, London, Souvenir Press.

Kanner, L. (1943) 'Autistic disturbances of affective contact', *Nervous Child* 2: 217–50.

Kay, R. H. and Mathews, D. R. (1972) 'On the existence in human auditory pathways of channels selectively tuned to the modulation present in frequency modulated tones', *Journal of Physiology* 225: 653–77.

Kirby, A. and Drew, S. (2003) *Guide to Dyspraxia: Developmental Communication Disorders*, London, David Fulton Publishers.

Knowles, W. and Masidlover, M. (1982) *Derbyshire Language Scheme*, Ripley, Derbyshire County Council.

—— and —— (1987) *Derbyshire Rapid Screening Test*, Ripley, Educational Psychology Service, Derbyshire County Council.

Landells, J. (1989) 'Assessment of semantics' in Grundy, K. (ed.) *Linguistics in Clinical Practice*, London, Whurr.

Law, J., Lindsay, G., Peacey, N. *et al.*, with Fitzgerald, L. (2000a) *Provision for Children with Speech and Language Needs in England and Wales: Facilitating Communication Between Education and Health Services*, London, DfEE Research Report RR239.

——, Parkinson, A. and Tamnhe, R. (eds) (2000b) *Communication Difficulties in Childhood*, Oxford, Radcliffe Medical Press.

Lawson, W. (1998) *Life Behind Glass: A Personal Account of Autistic Spectrum Disorder*, Lismore, Southern Cross University Press.

Lewis, A. (2004) 'And when did you last see your father? Exploring the views of children with learning difficulties/disabilities', *British Journal of Special Education* 31 (1): 3–9.

Lewis, J. and Wilson, D. (1998) *Pathways to Learning in Rett Syndrome*, London, David Fulton Publishers.

Liberman, I. Y., Shankweiler, D. and Liberman, A. M. (1989) 'The alphabetic principle and learning to read' in Shankweiler, D. and Liberman, I. Y. (eds) *Phonology and Reading Disability: Solving the Reading Puzzle*, Ann Arbor, MI, University of Michigan Press.

Locke, A., Ginsborg, J. and Peers, I. (2002) 'Development and disadvantage: implications for the early years and beyond', *International Journal of Language and Communication Disorders* 37 (1): 3–15.

Lord, C. and Schopler, E. (1987) 'Neurobiological implications of sex differences in autism' in Schopler, E. and Mesibov, G. (eds) *Neurobiological Issues in Autism*, New York, Plenum.

Lovaas, O. I. (1987) 'Behavioural treatment and normal intellectual and educational functioning in autistic children', *Journal of Consulting and Clinical Psychology*, 55: 3–9.

Marchant, R. and Cross, M. (2002) *How It Is*, London, National Society for the Prevention of Cruelty to Children.

Martin, D. (2000) *Teaching Children with Speech and Language Difficulties*, London, David Fulton Publishers.

—— and Miller, C. (2003) *Speech and Language Difficulties in the Classroom*, London, David Fulton Publishers.

—— and Reilly, O. (1995) 'Global language delay: analysis of a severe central auditory processing deficit' in Perkins, M. and Howard, S. (eds) *Case Studies in Clinical Linguistics*, London, Whurr.

Medical Research Council (2001) *Review of Autism Research: Epidemiology and Causes*, London, MRC (www.mrc.ac.uk).

Mesibov, G. and Howley, M. (2003) *Accessing the Curriculum for Pupils with Autistic Spectrum Disorders: Using the TEACCH Programme to Help Inclusion*, London, David Fulton Publishers.

Myles, B., Cook, K., Miller, N. *et al.* (2000a) *Asperger's Syndrome and Sensory Issues: Practical Solutions for Making Sense of the World*, Shawnee Mission, KS, Autism Asperger's Publishing Company.

—— Jones-Bock, S. and Simpson, R. (2000b) *Asperger's Syndrome Diagnostic Scale (ASDS)*, Oxford, Harcourt Assessment.

Newcomer, P. L. and Hammill, D. D. (1997) *Test of Language Development – Primary, Third Edition (TOLD-P:3)*, Oxford, The Psychological Corporation.

Nind, M. (1999) 'Intensive interaction and autism: a useful approach?', *British Journal of Special Education* 26 (2): 96–102.

Parker, M. (2000) 'Setting up a secondary base for secondary aged pupils with ASD within a mainstream secondary school', *Good Autism Practice Journal* 1 (2): 62–70.

Prevezer, W. (2000) 'Musical interaction and children with autism' in Powell, S. (ed.) *Helping Children with Autism to Learn*, London, David Fulton Publishers.

Prizant, B. M. and Wetherby, A. M. (1993) 'Communication in pre-school autistic children' in Schopler, E. *et al.* (eds) *Preschool Issues in Autism*, New York, Plenum.

Rapin, I. and Allen, D. (1987) 'Developmental dysphasia and autism in pre-school children: characteristics and subtypes' in *Proceedings of the First International Symposium on Specific Speech and Language Disorders in Children*, London, Association For All Speech Impaired Children.

Rinaldi, W. (1992/2001) *Social Use of Language Programme* (*SULP*), Windsor, NFER-Nelson.

—— (1996) *Understanding Ambiguity*, Windsor, NFER-Nelson.

Ripley, K., Barrett, J. and Fleming, P. (2001) *Inclusion for Children with Speech and Language Impairment*, London, David Fulton Publishers.

Rutter, M. (1996) 'Autism reseach: prospects and priorities', *Journal of Autism and Developmental Disorders* 26 (2): 257–75.

Schopler, E., Reichler, R. L. and Renner, B. R. (1988) *The Childhood Autism Rating Scale*, Los Angeles, CA, Western Psychological Services.

——, Van Bourgandien, M. and Bristol, M. (eds) (1993) *Pre-school Issues in Autism*, New York, Plenum.

Semel, E., Wiig, E. H. and Secord, W. A. (1997*) Clinical Evaluation of Language Fundamentals Test, Revised UK Edition* (*CELF-R*), Hove, Psychological Corporation.

Shaw, R. (2000) *Test of Word and Grammatical Awareness*, Windsor, NFER-Nelson.

Shields, J. (2001) The NAS EarlyBird programme: partnership with parents in early intervention', *Autism* 5 (1): 49–56.

Sherratt, D. and Donald, G. (2004) 'Connectedness: developing a shared construction of affect and cognition in children with autism', *British Journal of Special Education* 31 (1): 10–15.

Smith, B. R. and Leinonen, E. (1992) *Clinical Pragmatics: Unravelling the Complexities of Communication Failure*, London, Chapman and Hall.

Smith, C. (2003) *Writing and Developing Social Stories: Practical Interventions in Autism*, Oxford, Harcourt Assessment.

Sparrow, S. S., Balla, D. and Cicchetti, D. (1984) *Vineland Adaptive Behaviour Scale*, Circle Pines, MN, American Guidance Service.

Stackhouse, J. and Wells, B. (1997*) Children's Speech and Literacy Difficulties: A Psycholinguistic Framework*, London, Whurr Publishing.

Thompson, G. (2003) *Supporting Children with Communication Disorders: A Handbook for Teachers and Teaching Assistants*, London, David Fulton Publishers.

Van der Lely, H. (1994) 'Canonical linking rules: forward versus reverse linking in normally developing and language impaired children', *Cognition*: 51: 29–72.

Volkmar, F. R. and Nelson, D. (1990) 'Seizure disorders in autism', *Journal of American Academic Child and Adolescent Psychiatry* 29: 127–9.

Walker, M. (1980) *The Makaton Vocabulary (Revised)*, Camberley, The Makaton Vocabulary Development Project.

—— (ed.) (1993) *Makaton Resource Vocabulary: National Curriculum Series Part 1*, Camberley, Makaton Vocabulary Development Project.

Walley, A. C. (1993) 'The role of vocabulary development in children's spoken word recognition and segmentation ability', *Developmental Review* 13: 286–350.

Watson, I. (1991) 'Phonological processing in two languages' in Bailystok, E. (ed.) *Language Processing in Bilingual Children*, Cambridge, Cambridge University Press.

Wells, G. (1985) *Language Development in the Preschool Years*, Cambridge, Cambridge University Press.

Whitaker, P. (2001) *Challenging Behaviour and Autism*, London, National Autistic Society.

White, L. (1987) 'Against comprehensible input', *Applied Linguistics* 8 (2): 95–110.

Whittles, S. (1998) *Can You Hear Us?: Including the Views of Disabled Children and Young People*, London, Save the Children.

Wilson, M. S. (2000) *The Wilson Syntax Screening Test*, Oxford, The Psychological Corporation.

Wimpory, D. *et al.* (1995) 'Musical interaction therapy for children with autism: an illustrative case study with a 2 year follow up', Brief report, *Journal of Autism and Developmental Disorders* 25: 541–52.

Wing, L. (1996) *The Autistic Spectrum: A Guide for Parents and Professionals*, London, Constable.

—— and Gould, J. (1979) 'Severe impairments of social interaction and assorted abnormalities in children: epidemiology and classification, *Journal of Autism and Childhood Schizophrenia* 9: 11–29.

—— *et al.* (2002) The diagnostic interview for social and communication disorders: background, inter-rater reliability and clinical use', *Journal of Child Psychology and Psychiatry* 43: 307–25.

Wolff, S. (1998) 'Schizoid personality in childhood: the links with Asperger's syndrome, schizophrenia spectrum disorders and elective mutism' in Schopler, E., Mesibov, G. B. and Kunce, L. J. (eds) *Asperger's Syndrome or High Functioning Autism?* New York, Plenum Press, pp. 123–42.

Wray, A. (2001) 'Formulaic sequences in second language teaching: principle and practice', *Applied Linguistics* 21 (4): 463–89.

Index